SACK IT
AND
PACK IT

by

Darcy Williamson

—A MAVERICK PUBLICATION—

Maverick Publications
Drawer 5007 • Bend, Oregon 97701

Dedicated to
Grandmother Mabel

Illustrative Concepts
by
Cheryl Ann Eldridge

Special thanks to
Dorian Copenhaver, Chip Adams and Corrine Deapon

CONTENTS

Chapter 1

Bread Spreads and Fillings

Sandwiches can be as monotonous to make as they are to eat. Facing a slab of bologna and a jar of mayonnaise first thing in the morning can make even an optimist want to turn around and go back to bed. But don't reach for that peanut butter! Have some compassion for the hungry mouths that will groan, "Not that again!" several hours later. Imagine the guilt when you lunch on last night's tasty leftovers and visions of your family mouthing dry peanut butter sandwiches flash through your mind.

It takes only minutes to throw a few more slices of bacon into the skillet to use in Bacon-Celery Spread or a Bacon and Cream Cheese Sandwich. Toss in a few extra eggs when soft boiling for breakfast and allow the extras to hard-cook. Use them to whip up a Cheese-Egg Spread or Egg and Watercress Sandwiches. Unused spreads and fillings can be placed in tightly covered containers and refrigerated. The following filling and spread recipes include information on storage time.

I admit that the preparation of such delights as Clam and Cheese Spread or Deviled Tongue Spread can quickly lose appeal when approached at 7:15 in the morning. Most spreads and fillings can be prepared a day or more in advance, then all that is required during the morning ritual is smoothing a glob of the filling over bread and quickly hiding it beneath another slice. This small sacrifice will make a hit at noon.

1 Bread Spreads and Fillings

Don't be shy about using different breads for sandwiches. The family may be particularly fond of Grandpa Dick's Fluffy White Bread, but try raisin, wheat, rye, sourdough, English muffins, etc. and you may discover new favorites!

Bread Spreads & Fillings 2

SPREADS AND FILLINGS

BACON-CELERY SPREAD

9 slices bacon, cooked crisp and crumbled
3 Tbsp. mayonnaise
1½ cups finely diced celery

Combine bacon and celery; moisten with mayonnaise. Keeps up to 4 days.

BAKED BEAN AND RAISIN SPREAD

1 cup baked beans
½ cup raisins
1 Tbsp. horseradish
5 drops Worchestershire sauce
¼ cup minced green pepper
2 Tbsp. minced onion
2 Tbsp. mayonnaise

Mash beans. Soak raisins in hot water 10 minutes; drain and chop. Combine all ingredients and mix well. Extra good on whole wheat bread. Keeps up to 1 week.

BEET RELISH SPREAD

1 cup cooked beets, finely chopped
3 Tbsp. grated onion
2 hard-cooked eggs, finely chopped
½ Tbsp. vinegar
1 tsp. salt
¼ tsp. pepper
1 tsp. horseradish
2 Tbsp. mayonnaise

Combine all ingredients and chill overnight. Makes 5 sandwiches. Unused portion will keep up to 4 days.

CHEDDAR-PRUNE SPREAD

1 cup mashed, cooked prunes
1/4 cup finely chopped nut meats
1/2 cup grated cheddar cheese

Combine ingredients. Use fork to blend thoroughly. Spread between slices of buttered bread. Sandwiches freeze well. Unused spread keeps up to 6 days.

CHEESE-OLIVE SPREAD

2 cups sharp cheddar cheese, crumbled
1/2 cup mayonnaise
1/3 cup chopped black olives
1 pimiento, chopped
1/2 cup onion, minced
1 hard-cooked egg, chopped
1/4 tsp. salt

Beat cheese and mayonnaise with electric mixer until smooth. Add remaining ingredients and mix well. Keeps up to 1 week.

CHICKEN DELIGHT FILLING

1 cup diced cooked chicken
1/4 cup cottage cheese
1/2 cup drained crushed pineapple
Dash salt and pepper

Combine ingredients and mix well. Makes enough filling for 6 sandwiches. Unused filling keeps 3 to 4 days.

CLAM AND CHEESE SPREAD

1 pkg. (3-oz.) softened cream cheese
1 can (7-oz.) minced clams, drained
1 tsp. soy sauce
1 1/2 tsp. prepared mustard
1 Tbsp. minced onion

Mix all ingredients. Fills 4 sandwiches. Unused portion keeps up to 6 days.

Bread Spreads & Fillings 4

COLESLAW SPREAD

1 cup finely shredded cabbage
¼ cup minced green pepper
1 tsp. chili sauce
1 Tbsp. minced parsley
2 Tbsp. mayonnaise
1 Tbsp. lemon juice

Combine ingredients and mix well. Chill before spreading. Very good on Pumpernickle. Keeps up to 6 days.

COTTAGE CHEESE-FIG SPREAD

½ lb. cottage cheese
3 Tbsp. mayonnaise
2 Tbsp. chopped dried figs

Blend well and spread between slices of bread. Unused portions keep up to 4 days.

COTTAGE CHEESE FILLING

1 cup cottage cheese
2 Tbsp. finely chopped radish
2 Tbsp. minced cucumber
1 Tbsp. finely sliced green onion

Mix all ingredients together and spread between whole wheat bread. Makes 4 to 6 sandwiches. Keeps up to 3 days.

DEVILED HAM SANDWICH SPREAD

1 can (4½-oz.) deviled ham
2 Tbsp. mayonnaise
1 Tbsp. chopped sweet pickle
1 Tbsp. chopped pimento
½ Tbsp. chopped celery

Combine all ingredients and mix well. Makes 3 sandwiches. Unused portion keeps up to five days.

DEVILED TONGUE SPREAD

2 cans (3-oz. each) deviled tongue
2/3 cup piccalilli, drained
1/4 cup minced celery
2 Tbsp. mayonnaise

Combine all ingredients and mix well. Chill. Makes 5 sandwiches. Unused portion will keep up to 5 days.

GUACAMOLE FILLING

1 medium-sized avocado, peeled and pitted
1/2 Tbsp. chili salsa
1 tsp. lemon juice
1/4 cup grated Cheddar cheese
2 tsp. mayonnaise

Mash avocado. Add remaining ingredients. Good on whole grain bread. Does not keep well.

LIVER-CHEESE SPREAD

1/4 lb. chicken livers
1 Tbsp. margarine
3 Tbsp. blue cheese, crumbled
1/4 tsp. onion powder
Salt and pepper to taste

Saute livers in margarine, cool and chop fine. Add remaining ingredients and spread between buttered bread slices. Makes 3 to 4 sandwiches. Keeps up to 4 days.

LIVERWURST SANDWICH SPREAD

1/2 lb. liverwurst
2 Tbsp. prepared horseradish
1 tsp. prepared mustard
2 Tbsp. chopped onion
Dash salt and pepper

Mash liverwurst thoroughly. Blend in remaining ingredients and mix well.

Bread Spreads & Fillings　　**6**

MINCED CARROT SPREAD

4 medium-sized carrots
½ green pepper
3 stalks celery
¼ cup walnut meats
1 Tbsp. horseradish
3 Tbsp. mayonnaise
Lemon juice to taste

Put vegetables and nuts through food grinder, using finest blade, twice. Mix with horseradish and mayonnaise. Add lemon juice. Chill before spreading.

PEANUT BUTTER-HAM SPREAD

¼ cup creamy peanut butter
1 can (3-oz.) ham spread
3 Tbsp. margarine
1 Tbsp. prepared mustard
¼ Tbsp. Worcestershire sauce

Mix peanut butter, ham and mayonnaise until well blended. Add mustard and Worcestershire sauce. Mix to a paste and spread on bread. Unused portion keeps up to six days.

PEANUT BUTTER PLUS FILLING

½ cup peanut butter
¾ cup carrot, finely shredded
¼ cup dried currents
3 Tbsp. mayonnaise

Combine all ingredients and spread on buttered bread (raisin is particularly good). Filling keeps up to five days.

Bread Spreads & Fillings

SALMON SPREAD

¼ cup margarine
1 tsp. lemon juice
1 can (7¾-Oz.) salmon, drained, or
¾ cup cooked flaked salmon
¼ cup ripe diced olives
2 Tbsp. minced celery
½ tsp. prepared horseradish

Combine all ingredients and mix well. Keeps up to 4 days.

SAN FRANCISCO SPREAD

½ cup finely shredded iceberg lettuce
3-oz. salami, diced
¼ cup finely diced radishes
1½ Tbsp. sweet pickle relish

Combine ingredients and mix well. Spread on buttered bread. Unused portions will keep 2 days.

TUNA-COTTAGE CHEESE SPREAD

1 can (6-oz.) tuna, drained
1 Tbsp. mayonnaise
½ cup creamed cottage cheese
3 Tbsp. snipped fresh chives
¼ tsp. seasoned pepper
Dash salt

Combine all ingredients in bowl. Chill. Spread on buttered bread. Unused portion will keep 3 days.

TUNA-EGG SALAD SPREAD

1 cup canned tuna
2 hard-cooked eggs, chopped
2 Tbsp. minced parsley
1 Tbsp. minced onion
1/2 cup chopped celery
1 apple, grated
2 Tbsp. horseradish
2 Tbsp. mayonnaise
Dash salt and pepper

Combine all ingredients, mix thoroughly. Chill, Keeps up to 3 days.

TUNA ORIENTAL SPREAD

1 can (6 1/2-Oz.) tuna, drained
1/4 cup chopped water chestnuts
2 Tbsp. canned crushed pineapple
2/3 Tbsp. curry powder
1/4 cup mayonnaise
Dash salt

Combine tuna, chestnuts and pineapple. Mix together curry, mayonnaise and salt; stir into tuna mixture. Keeps up to 5 days.

TURKEY-CUCUMBER FILLING

1 cup diced turkey
3/4 cup chopped cucumber
Dash salt and pepper
1/4 cup mayonnaise

Combine ingredients and mix well. Makes 5 sandwiches. Unused filling will keep up to 3 days.

TURKEY-RELISH FILLING

> 1 cup cooked diced turkey
> ¾ cup diced celery
> 3 Tbsp. sweet pickle relish
> 1 hard-cooked egg, chopped
> ¼ tsp. salt
> Dash of pepper
> ¼ cup mayonnaise

Combine ingredients and mix well. Makes 6 sandwiches. Keeps up to 4 days.

TURKEY-SCALLION FILLING

> 1 cup cooked diced turkey
> ½ cup chopped scallions
> 1 Tbsp. Worcestershire sauce
> Dash salt and pepper
> ¼ cup mayonnaise

Combine ingredients and mix well. Makes enough filling for 5 sandwiches. Unused filling will keep up to 4 days.

VEGETARIAN SANDWICH SPREAD

> 14 green peppers
> 8 medium onions
> 6 red peppers
> 8 green tomatoes
> 1½ cups vinegar
> 1½ cups brown sugar
> 4 Tbsp. prepared mustard
> 6 Tbsp. flour
> 1 qt. mayonnaise

Grind vegetables together and scald in boiling water for 10 minutes. Drain well. Put in large pan and add vinegar and sugar; cook for 8 minutes. Make paste of mustard and flour; add to ingredients. Cook 3 more minutes; add mayonnaise and cook until desired thickness (about 4 minutes). Pour into pint jars and seal.

SANDWICHES

BACON AND CREAM CHEESE SANDWICHES

4 slices whole grain bread
2 Tbsp. softened margarine
3 slices bacon
½ 8-0z. pkg. cream cheese

Fry bacon crisp; crumble and mix with cream cheese. Spread bread with margarine and fill with filling. Makes 2 sandwiches. May be wrapped in foil and frozen.

BANANA-NUT SANDWICHES

1 banana
½ cup chopped walnuts
Dash sugar
Dash nutmeg
4 slices whole wheat bread

Mash bananas; add nuts, sugar, and nutmeg. Spread bread with mayonnaise; add filling and lettuce, if desired, between slices. Makes 4 sandwiches.

Bread Spreads & Fillings

BOLOGNA-CHEESE GRINDERS

3-oz. bologna
2 slices pimento cheese
¼ cup onion, chopped
3 small sweet pickles
2 Tbsp. green pepper, chopped
1½ Tbsp. mayonnaise
1 tsp. prepared mustard
3 sourdough rolls, halved
Lettuce
1 tomato, sliced

Grind together bologna, cheese, onion and pickles. Add green pepper, mayonnaise and mustard. Spread each roll with ¼ cup filling, top with lettuce and tomato. Cover with top half of roll. (Lettuce and tomato may be packed separately and added to grinder at serving time to avoid possible sogginess.)

BOLOGNA CLUB SANDWICHES

4 slices white bread
¼ cup mayonnaise
¼ tsp. curry powder
4 slices bologna
½ medium cucumber, sliced
4 slices Swiss cheese
Prepared mustard
Lettuce
2 slices whole wheat bread

Add curry to mayonnaise. Spread on white bread. On two slices, stack half the bologna, cucumber and cheese. Spread cheese with mustard; top with lettuce and whole wheat bread. Spread with curried mayonnaise; stack remaining fillings, lettuce and bread. Quarter sandwiches and secure with olive-topped toothpick. Makes 2.

CHEESE AND NUT SANDWICH

Pimiento cheese spread
Pecans, coarsely chopped
Lettuce

Spread 1 slice of buttered bread with pimiento cheese. Sprinkle thickly with nuts. Lay on lettuce half (or pack separately to add to sandwich later); top with another bread slice.

CHICKEN SALAD SANDWICH

4 slices white bread
2 Tbsp. mayonnaise
½ cup ground cooked chicken
1 Tbsp. pickle relish
2 Tbsp. cream cheese
½ Tbsp. grated onion

Spread bread slices with mayonnaise. Combine chicken with relish, cream cheese and onion. Spread on 2 bread slices; top with remaining slices. Keeps up to 5 days.

CRAB MEAT SANDWICHES

1 cup crab meat
¼ cup mayonnaise
20 thin slices of cucumber
4 slices whole wheat bread
Soft margarine

Combine crab and mayonnaise. Spread bread with margarine; cover half with crab mixture and cucumber slices. Cover with remaining slices of bread.

CURRIED BACON-BANANA SANDWICHES

4 slices bacon
2 Tbsp. mayonnaise
½ tsp. lemon juice
⅛ tsp. curry powder
1 medium-sized banana, diced
4 slices bread

Cook bacon until crisp; drain and crumble. Mix next 3 ingredients, add to banana and mix carefully. Fold in bacon. Spread between bread. Makes 2 sandwiches.

DEVILED HAM AND CUCUMBER SANDWICHES

2 cucumbers
1 small onion
French dressing
1 small can (4½-Oz.) deviled ham

Slice cucumber and onion thin; marinate in French dressing 30 minutes. Cover 1 slice of bread with cucumber and onion and a second slice of bread with deviled ham. Press slices together. Makes 3 sandwiches.

EGG AND CUCUMBER SANDWICHES

4 hard-cooked eggs, mashed
¼ cup finely chopped cucumber
3 Tbsp. Thousand Island dressing

Mix ingredients together and spread on white bread. Makes three sandwiches.

EGG AND WATERCRESS SANDWICHES

4 hard-cooked eggs, mashed
3 Tbsp. mayonnaise
1 cup watercress, chopped

Combine ingredients and mix well. Spread thickly between slices of buttered bread. Makes 3 sandwiches.

Bread Spreads & Fillings   **14**

FRUIT AND COTTAGE CHEESE SANDWICHES

1 cup creamed cottage cheese
1/4 cup mayonnaise
1/2 cup drained crushed pineapple
1/2 cup chopped dates
2 Tbsp. pecans, finely chopped

Combine ingredients. Chill and serve between slices of whole wheat bread. Makes 5 sandwiches. Extra filling keeps 3 to 5 days.

HAM 'N MARMALADE SANDWICHES

4 slices ham
2 Tbsp. orange marmalade
8 slices raisin bread
Margarine

Spread margarine on bread slices; top half with ham. Spread with marmalade. Place remaining slices of bread on top. Unused sandwiches may be frozen for up to three months.

HAM AND SWISS SANDWICHES

4 slices rye bread
2 Tbsp. softened margarine
1 Tbsp. chutney
1/2 Tbsp. Dijon mustard
6 thin slices ham
2 slices Swiss cheese

Blend together margarine, chutney and mustard. Spread on bread slices. Place 3 slices of ham and 1 slice of cheese on each of 2 slices of bread. Top with remaining bread slices.

ROQUEFORT AND APPLE SANDWICHES

1 cup Roquefort cheese, crumbled
4 Tbsp. margarine
1 cup tart grated apple

Combine ingredients and mix well. Spread between rye or whole wheat bread. Makes 4 to 6 sandwiches. Filling keeps 2 to 3 days.

15   Bread Spreads & Fillings

ROQUEFORT-LIVERWURST SANDWICHES

1 medium-sized Bermuda onion
¼ cup wine vinegar
¼ cup Roquefort cheese, crumbled
2 Tbsp. mayonnaise
8 slices liverwurst
8 slices rye bread

Thinly slice onion; marinate in vinegar 15 minutes. Combine cheese with mayonnaise and spread on four bread slices, place 2 slices liverwurst on each. Drain onions and arrange on liverwurst; top with remaining bread.

SALAMI HEROES

3 hard-cooked eggs, chopped
2 Tbsp. mayonnaise
Dash crushed red pepper
¼ cup cucumber, finely chopped
3 hero rolls
Margarine
Lettuce leaves
9 slices salami
9 slices tomatoes
Anchovy fillets

Mix together first 5 ingredients. Split rolls and spread with margarine. Fill with layers of lettuce, egg mixture, salami, tomatoes and anchovies. You may wish to pack lettuce and tomatoes separately, to be added later. Makes 3.

SARDINE SANDWICHES

1 tin sardines in oil
1 small Bermuda onion
1 tsp. Dijon mustard
2 Tbsp. mayonnaise
4 slices whole wheat bread

Drain sardines, set aside. Cut onions into ¼" thick slices. Combine mustard and mayonnaise. Spread bread slices with mustard-mayonnaise mixture. Arrange sardines and onion slices on 2 slices of bread, top with remaining bread slices.

SARDINE AND EGG SANDWICH

4 hard-cooked eggs, riced
⅔ cup sardines, mashed
3 Tbsp. French dressing
2 Tbsp. lemon juice

Combine ingredients and mix well. Spread between slices of buttered rye bread. Makes 4 sandwiches.

SAVORY MEAT LOAF SANDWICHES

⅓ cup fine dry bread crumbs
1 cup milk
1 small onion, minced
1½ tsp. margarine
1 lb. ground beef
1 carrot, grated
1 egg
1 Tbsp. chili sauce
½ tsp. salt
¼ tsp. pepper
½ tsp. ginger
½ tsp. curry powder
1 tsp. anchovy paste (optional)

Mix crumbs and milk in bowl. Saute' onion in margarine. Add onion and remaining ingredients, except mustard, to crumb mixture and blend well. Shape into loaf. Spread thin coat of mustard on top. Bake in 350° F. oven 60 minutes. Cool; then chill before slicing. Extra slices may be frozen.

To make sandwiches, place thin slices on mayonnaised bread. Salt and pepper before adding another bread slice.

SHRIMP SANDWICHES

½ lb. cooked, peeled shrimp, finely chopped
3 stalks celery, diced
1 apple, cored and chopped
1 Tbsp. catsup
3 Tbsp. mayonnaise
8 slices whole wheat bread
Softened margarine

Combine shrimp, celery, apple, catsup and mayonnaise. Spread margarine on bread; spread half with filling and top with remaining bread.

TONGUE-CURRY SANDWICH

6 thin slices of tongue
¼ cup mayonnaise
1 tsp. curry powder
Lettuce leaves
4 slices white bread

Combine mayonnaise with curry. Spread on bread. Arrange tongue on slices of bread. Cover with remaining slices. Lettuce is best wrapped separately and added just before sandwiches are eaten. Makes 2 sandwiches.

TURKEY-SWISS SANDWICHES

¼ Tbsp. mayonnaise
½ tsp. prepared mustard
1 cup diced chicken
½ cup shredded Swiss cheese
8 slices raisin bread
Softened margarine

Combine mayonnaise, mustard, chicken and cheese. Spread with margarine before adding filling. Makes 4 sandwiches.

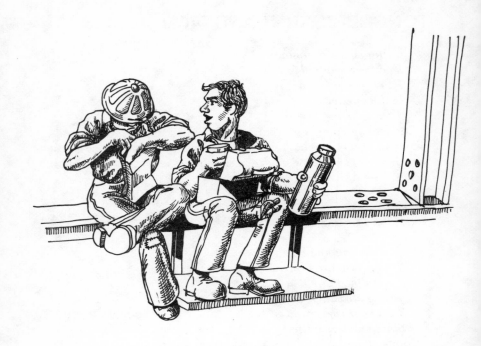

Chapter 2

From the Freezer to the Sack

Are you one of those reluctant risers who plot and scheme to extract a few more minutes of oblivion out of the morning? If twenty minutes to nine finds you scurrying about the house attending to last minute details, this chapter is for you.

By using your freezer to store make-ahead foods, you can have lunch thrown together in two minutes. The frozen lunch will thaw by noon. Can you imagine the expressions of fellow workers as you unpack your Chilled-Avocado-Sour Cream Soup, Cold Curried Chicken Loaf with a side of Relish Salad and Cheesecake for dessert? They'll think you're a wizard (or that you have an ambitious live-in).

A little advanced planning and food preparation is all that is required (come on now, you knew there had to be a catch somewhere). Let's start with the Chilled Avocado-Sour Cream Soup. All the ingredients are dumped into a blender and blended until smooth; then poured into pint jars (leaving 1" at the top for expansion), secured with lids, labeled and frozen. Simple. The Cold Curried Chicken Loaf may be prepared and served for supper. The left-over loaf may then be chilled, sliced, wrapped, labeled and stacked in the freezer. This is easier than you thought, right?

The following recipes will give you a multitude of ideas

for freezer stockpiling, but before you begin, here are a few standard freezing facts to freshen your memory:

1. When preparing sandwiches for the freezer, spread butter or margarine on both bread slices, being careful to cover entire surface area.
2. Do not use mayonnaise, egg whites, jam, jelly or fresh vegetables on sandwiches prepared for the freezer.
3. Lettuce and tomato slices cannot be frozen but may be added when the sandwich is partially or wholly thawed.
4. Sandwiches should not be kept in the freezer over 2 months.
5. Foods may be wrapped in freezer paper, plastic wrap or bags, or aluminum foil. It is necessary to exclude as much air as possible before securing with freezer tape, metal or plastic twists or rubber bands.
6. Labels should include name of food, date it was frozen and freezer life; plus any serving suggestions which may be helpful.
7. Plastic containers used for freezing should be filled ½" to 1" from top of container to allow for expansion. Glass containers should have a little more room for expansion (¾" for pints and 1½" for quarts).

Start stockpiling and enjoy those stolen moments of sleep!

From Freezer to Sack

MAIN COURSES

BROWN BREAD-CREAM CHEESE ROUNDS

1 cup raisins
1 1/2 cups water
3 Tbsp. butter
1/2 tsp. salt
1 cup sugar
1 egg
1 3/4 cup flour
2 tsp. baking soda
1 tsp. baking powder
1 cup bran flakes
1 tsp. vanilla

Combine raisins, water, butter and salt; bring to boil in saucepan and boil 2 minutes. Cool and drain liquid. Reserve drained liquid. Beat together sugar and egg. Add flour, soda and baking powder. Alternate flour and liquid. Add bran, raisins and vanilla. Mix well. Pour batter into 3 well greased 1 lb. cans and bake in 350°F. oven for 50 to 60 minutes. Cool in cans 10 minutes. Let stand 24 hours before slicing. Spread slice with softened cream cheese and top with another bread slice. Wrap each sandwich separately and freeze. Makes 6 to 8 servings.

From Freezer to Sack

CHEESY HASH TURNOVERS

2 pkg. (10 per package) buttermilk refrigerator biscuits
¾ cup shredded cheddar cheese
1 can (#303) corned beef hash
1 Tbsp. prepared mustard
½ tsp. Worcestershire sauce
Hot Chinese mustard

Separate biscuits and roll out thin. Mix remaining ingredients (except Chinese mustard). Place 2 Tbsp. of mixture in center of each biscuit. Fold over and seal edges with fork. Cut 2 vents in top. Place on king sheet and bake 8 minutes at 425°F. Wrap each separately and freeze. Serve chilled with Chinese mustard. Makes 4 to 5 servings.

CHILLED AVOCADO-SOUR CREAM SOUP

1 can (10½-oz.) condensed beef broth
2 avocados, peeled and pitted
½ cup sour cream
1 green onion, sliced
1 tsp. salt
1 Tbsp. lemon juice
2 drops hot pepper sauce

Put all ingredients in blender container and blend until smooth. Pour into pint jars, secure lids, label and freeze. Keeps up to 3 months.

COLD CURRIED CHICKEN LOAF

3 lbs. chicken backs and necks
2 Tbsp. butter
Salt
1 stalk celery, cut up
1 medium onion, sliced
2 small carrots, cut up
4 whole peppercorns
1½ Tbsp. curry powder
1 can (13-oz.) evaporated milk

In Dutch oven, brown chicken in butter. Add 1 tsp. salt, 2 cups water and next 4 ingredients. Bring to boil; cover and simmer 1½ hours. Stir in curry and cool chicken in broth. Remove meat, discarding skin and bones. Set meat aside. Stir evaporated milk into broth and simmer 5 minutes. Add salt and pepper to taste. Strain broth and discard cooked vegetables. Arrange meat in 1½ quart glass loaf pan and pour broth over top. Refrigerate overnight to gel. Invert on cold platter and slice into 1" thick slices. Wrap serving-sized portions in freezer wrap and freeze. To serve, place frozen wrapped portions in paper bowl and pack in lunch sack.

CHILLED CHICKEN MARQUERITE

2½ lb. chicken breasts, skinned and split
½ cup olive oil
1½ tsp. salt
½ tsp. freshly ground pepper
2 tsp. paprika
1 tsp. tarragon
¼ cup butter
2 cups dry sherry

Pour oil into flat baking dish. Add chicken breasts in single layer. Sprinkle with seasonings and herbs and dot with butter. Pour sherry over chicken and bake 350°F. for 40 minutes, basting frequently. Cool. Wrap pieces of chicken individually, label and freeze. To use, remove freezer wrapping and rewrap in plastic wrap. Place in lunch bag. Stores up to 3 months.

From Freezer to Sack

COLD POACHED FISH WITH COCKTAIL SAUCE

4 cups water
1 tsp. salt
1 lb. fish fillets (halibut or ocean perch), thawed
1/2 cup catsup
2 Tbsp. horseradish
1 Tbsp. lemon juice
Dash of pepper

Boil water and salt; add fish, cover and simmer 3 to 6 minutes until fish flakes easily with fork. Chill.

To prepare sauce, combine remaining ingredients. Spoon over chilled fish and mix well. Pack into serving-sized containers and freeze. Stores up to 2½ months and makes 3 to 4 servings.

CORNED BEEF SANDWICHES

2 cups ground cooked corned beef
1/4 cup diced dill pickle
1/4 tsp. hot pepper sauce
1 tsp. prepared mustard
2 tsp. prepared horseradish
3 Tbsp. margarine

Blend all ingredients together. Spread filling on 8 slices of rye bread, top with another slice of bread. Wrap each sandwich individually, label and freeze. Makes 8 sandwiches and stores up to 2 months.

CRAB OR SHRIMP SALAD

1 pkg. (8-oz.) cream cheese
1 can (10½-oz.) tomato soup
2 Tbsp. unflavored gelatin
½ cup cold water
2 Tbsp. sherry wine
1 tsp. onion salt
1 cup mayonnaise
¾ cup finely diced celery
¾ cup finely diced green pepper
¾ lb. crab meat or shrimp

Soften cream cheese, then blend with soup in top of double boiler. Stir over boiling water until mixture is hot. Meanwhile, soften gelatin in cold water. Add to cream cheese-soup misture and stir to dissolve gelatin. Stir in sherry and onion salt. Cool. Fold in mayonnaise, celery and green pepper. Add crab or shrimp and mix gently. Spoon into individual molds, secure with freezer wrap, label and freeze. To serve, line paper bowl with lettuce, unmold salad onto lettuce at lunch time. Keeps up to 2 months.

CREAM CHEESE FILLED ONION-CHEDDAR MUFFINS

2 cups packaged biscuit mix
1 tsp. onion salt
¾ cup shredded cheddar cheese
1 can (3½-oz.) French fried onions, crumbled
1 egg
1 cup milk
3 pkg. (3-oz. each) cream cheese

Mix together all ingredients, except cream cheese, and beat vigorously 1 minute. Fill 16 greased muffin tins ⅔ full. Bake in 400°F. oven 20 minutes. Cool; split and spread with cream cheese. Wrap each muffin individually and freeze. Keeps up to 3 months.

FRACADELLER

2 lbs. fine ground round
2 medium onions, minced
6 Tbsp. dried bread crumbs
2 cups milk
1 cup thick cream
2 eggs, beaten
1 tsp. salt
½ tsp. pepper
⅔ cup margarine

Add bread crumbs to meat and mix well. Beat in milk and cream. Add eggs, salt and pepper. Heat margarine in skillet. Mold meat into oblong shapes and saute in margarine until cooked. Cool. Wrap and freeze in serving-sized portions. Keeps up to 3 months.

ICED CREAM OF VEGETABLE SOUP

1 cup diced raw potato
¼ cup sliced green onion
1 cup raw peas (fresh or frozen)
¼ cup sliced celery
1½ cups chicken broth
1 cup light cream
Salt and pepper
Parsley

Place vegetables and broth in saucepan. Cover and simmer over medium heat until tender. Cool slightly, then whirl in blender until smooth. Stir in cream. Season with salt and pepper, then pour into pint jars with tight fitting lids. Sprinkle with parsley, close jars and freeze. Keeps up to 2 months.

LEMON CHICKEN

2 cut-up fryers
Salt and pepper
1/2 cup margarine, melted
1 cup frozen lemonade, thawed
6 cups corn flake crumbs

Rinse chicken in cold water, pat dry, sprinkle with salt and pepper and place chicken in bowl. Pour lemonade over. Stir to coat all pieces. Let stand at room temperature for 1 hour. Drain and roll pieces in crumbs, coating well. Brush shallow baking pan with margarine. Place pieces of chicken in shallow baking pan in single layer. Drizzle with remaining margarine. Bake at 350°F. 2 hours. Cool. Place several pieces into freezer bags and freeze. Keeps up to 2½ months.

LEMON SALMON STEAKS

3 salmon steaks
1 cup lemon juice
1/3 cup sliced green onion
2 Tbsp. cooking oil
2 tsp. snipped parsley
2 tsp. finely chopped celery leaves
1/2 Tbsp. sugar
1 tsp. dry mustard
1/2 tsp. salt
Dash cayenne

Poach steaks in simmering water 5 to 7 minutes. Carefully remove steaks with slotted spoon and place in shallow pan. Combine remaining ingredients and pour over steaks. Chill over-night. Drain steaks, wrap, label and freeze. Keeps up to 4 months.

From Freezer to Sack

RAISIN NUT BREAD ROUNDS

1 1/2 cup raisins
1 cup water
1 egg, beaten
3/4 cup sugar
1/2 tsp. vanilla
1 1/2 cups flour
1 tsp. baking powder
1/4 tsp. baking soda
Dash salt
1/2 cup chopped walnuts
Peanut butter
Cream cheese

In saucepan, combine raisins and water; bring to boil. Remove from heat; cool to room temperature. Mix together egg, sugar and vanilla; stir in raisin mixture. Sift together flour, baking powder, soda and salt. Add to raisin mixture, beating well. Stir in nuts. Pour into 2 greased and floured 16-oz. fruit or vegetable cans. Bake 350°F. 50 to 60 minutes. Cool. Remove bread from cans, slice, then spread with peanut butter and cream cheese; sandwich spread rounds with another round. Wrap, label and freeze. Keeps up to 4 months.

ROAST BEEF SANDWICHES

1 lb. sliced cooked roast beef
1 pkg. (3-oz.) cream cheese
1/4 cup catsup
2 Tbsp. prepared mustard
1 Tbsp. prepared horseradish
1/4 cup green onions, thinly sliced
12 slices caraway rye bread

Blend together cream cheese, catsup, mustard and horseradish. Stir in green onion. Spread slices of bread with cream cheese mixture. Arrange slices of roast beef on 6 slices of bread and cover with remaining slices. Wrap individually, label and freeze. Makes 6 sandwiches and keeps up to 2 months.

From Freezer to Sack

SAVORY MEAT LOAF

1 1/2 cups soft bread crumbs
1 can (8-oz.) tomato sauce
1 egg
1/2 tsp. salt
1 tsp. Worcestershire sauce
1 cup grated onion
2 lbs. hamburger

Combine all ingredients and mix well. Spoon meat mixture into greased 9" x 5" x 4" pan and smooth top. Bake at 375°F. for 1 hour and 15 minutes. Cool. Cut into serving-sized slices and wrap and label each slice. Freeze. To use, place needed portions in lunch box. Good with mustard, horseradish or catsup (packed in small tightly sealed plastic containers). Keeps up to 2 months.

STUFFED BUNWICHES

6 hard-cooked egg yolks, riced
  (use whites in salads, etc.)
1 can (12-oz.) corned beef, chopped
1/4 cup sweet pickle relish
1/4 cup mayonnaise
1 Tbsp. prepared mustard
Salt and pepper
12 hot dog buns
Soft margarine

Combine eggs, corned beef, relish, mayonnaise, mustard, salt and pepper. Cut off tops of buns and hollow out slightly. Spread margarine on the inside of each bun, being careful to cover entire surface. Fill with corned beef mixture; replace tops. Seal each tightly in foil and freeze. Keeps up to 3 months.

From Freezer to Sack

SUPER DAGWOOD

1 12" loaf unsliced dark rye bread
¼ cup margarine, softened
8 slices cooked ham
4 slices provolone or Swiss cheese
⅓ cup Thousand Island dressing
8 slices cooked turkey
4 large slices salami

Cut loaf lengthwise into 2 slices; spread all cut surfaces with margarine. Place bottom slice on bread board and top with ham and cheese slices. Spread with ½ of the dressing.

Place second slice of bread on top of ham and cheese, top with turkey and salami slices and remaining dressing. Top with last ⅓ bread. Skewer with picks and cut into four sections. Wrap each tightly in foil, label and freeze. Keeps up to 2 months.

SWEET AND SOUR CHICKEN WINGS

16 chicken wings
⅔ cup soy sauce
⅔ cup freshly squeezed lemon juice
⅔ cup honey
3 cloves garlic, crushed
6 Tbsp. peanut oil

Mix soy sauce with lemon juice, honey and garlic in large bowl. Add chicken wings. Cover and marinate in refrigerator overnight, turning occasionally. Drain wings. Heat oil in skillet over medium heat. Cook wings in oil, turning often, for 25 minutes or until wings are cooked throughout. Remove from skillet and drain on paper towels. Cool. Wrap serving-sized portions in freezer wrap, seal, label and freeze. Stores up to 3 months.

SIDE DISHES

APPLESAUCE

16 sour apples, pared, cored and quartered
2 cups water
2 cups sugar
1/2 tsp. ground cinnamon
1/4 tsp. ground nutmeg

Put all ingredients in kettle and simmer gently until apples are cooked. Add more water if needed. Put through food mill or strainer. Cool. Spoon into serving-sized containers with tight fitting lids. Wrap freezer tape around seam of lid to seal. Label and date. Keeps up to 8 months.

BONANZA SALAD

1 can kidney beans, drained
1 can cut wax beans, drained
1 can cut green beans, drained
1 can chick peas, drained
1/2 medium-sized red onion, cut into thin slices
1/2 cup sugar
1/2 cup salad oil
1 tsp. salt
1/2 tsp. dry mustard
1/2 tsp. dried basil leaves
1/4 tsp. pepper

Combine beans and onion in bowl. Mix remaining ingredients well and pour over beans. Stir to coat beans with dressing. Spoon beans into individual serving containers with tight fitting lids. Pour dressing over beans, seal, label and freeze. Keeps up to 3 months.

From Freezer to Sack

CRANBERRY SAUCE

4 cups cranberries
2 cups sugar
1 cup water

Combine cranberries with sugar and water in saucepan. Bring to boil and cook, stirring occasionally, until all cranberries have popped open. Chill. Spoon into individual serving containers with tight fitting lids. Seal lid seam with freezer tape and freeze. Keeps up to 8 months.

GOLDEN FRUIT COMPOTE

1 can (2 lb.) pear slices, undrained
¾ cup orange juice
1 cup dried apricots
¼ cup light colored raisins
⅛ tsp. ground cinnamon
⅛ tsp. ground nutmeg

Combine ingredients in saucepan. Cover and cook over low heat 2 hours. Cool. Spoon into individual serving containers with tight fitting lids. Seal, label and freeze.

MELON COCKTAIL

1 honeydew, cantaloupe, or other firm melon
½ cup sugar
½ cup water

Boil together sugar and water; cool. Remove seeds and rind from melon and cut meat into cubes. Place cubes into individual serving containers with tight fitting lids. Pour cool sugar-water syrup over melon; close containers, seal and freeze. Keeps up to 6 months.

PEACHES IN SYRUP

1½ lb. peaches
1 Tbsp. lemon juice
½ cup water
½ cup sugar

Blanch peaches 1 minute in boiling water, peel and pit. Slice fruit and sprinkle with lemon juice. Boil together sugar and water. Cool. Pour over peaches. Pack in individual containers, seal with freezer tape, label and freeze. Keeps up to 8 months.

PICKLED BEETS

1½ lb. young beets
Sweet pickle juice

Wash and trim tops of beets, leaving 1" of stem and root. Cook in boiling water until tender (25 to 50 minutes). Cool. Peel and slice.

Place sliced beets in individual containers. Pour sweet pickle juice over each serving to barely cover beets. Cover containers with lids and seal seam with freezer tape. Label and freeze. Keeps up to 6 months.

RELISH SALAD

1 Tbsp. unflavored gelatin
¼ cup cold water
1 cup prepared chili sauce
1 cup cottage cheese
¼ cup pickle relish, drained
½ cup prepared mayonnaise
¼ tsp. salt
¾ cup heavy cream, whipped

Soften gelatin in cold water. Dissolve over hot water. Mix together with chili sauce, cottage cheese, relish, mayonnaise, salt and whipped cream. Spoon into 8" x 8" x 2" pan. Freeze until firm enough to cut into squares. Wrap each square individually, label and freeze. Keeps up to 6 weeks.

From Freezer to Sack

RHUBARB SAUCE

3 cups rhubarb, cut into 1" pieces
1 cup sugar
½ cup water
1 Tbsp. grated orange rind

Combine ingredients in saucepan. Cover and cook over low heat until mixture comes to a full boil, stirring occasionally. Chill.

Spoon into individual serving containers with tight fitting lids and seal seam with freezer tape. Freeze. Keeps up to 6 months.

APPLE ROLLS

1½ cups milk, scalded
1 cup sugar
½ cup margarine
1 tsp. salt
2 pkg. active dry yeast
¼ cup lukewarm water
2 eggs, beaten
7 cups sifted flour
1 tsp. nutmeg
1 cup applesauce
2 Tbsp. brown flour
1 cup raisins
2 Tbsp. melted margarine
2 Tbsp. sugar
1 tsp. nutmeg

Combine milk with ½ cup sugar, margarine and salt, cool to lukewarm. Soften yeast in water, then beat, with eggs, into milk mixture. Add 2 cups flour. Cover and let rise in warm place until bubbly. Add remaining ½ cup sugar, flour and nutmeg. Mix well. Cover and let rise until double in bulk (1½ to 2 hours).

Turn dough onto lightly floured board and roll ¼" thick. Cut into 4" squares. Combine applesauce with brown sugar and raisins. Put spoonful in center of each square. Bring corners up to center and pinch edges together to seal. Place on greased cookie sheet. Brush with melted margarine and sprinkle with sugar which has been mixed with nutmeg. Let rise until double in bulk, Bake at 375°F. for 25 minutes. Cool. Wrap each individually and freeze. Keeps up to 3 months.

APRICOT-CREAM CHEESE BREAD

2 pkg. (3-oz.) cream cheese, softened
1/3 cup sugar
1 Tbsp. flour
1 egg
2 tsp. grated orange peel
1 egg, slightly beaten
1/2 cup orange juice
1 pkg. (17-oz.) apricot-nut quick bread mix

Combine cream cheese, sugar and flour; beat in 1 egg and orange peel. Set aside. Combine slightly beaten egg, juice and 1/2 cup water. Add bread mix, stirring until moistened. Turn 2/3 of the apricot batter into greased and floured 9" x 5" x 3" pan. Pour cheese mixture on top.

Spoon on remaining batter. Bake at 350°F. 1 hour. Cool 10 minutes before removing from pan. Cool completely before slicing. Wrap, label and freeze slices. Keeps up to 5 months.

BANANA CAKE

2 1/4 cups sifted cake flour
2 tsp. baking powder
3/4 tsp. baking soda
1/2 tsp. salt
1 1/2 cups sugar
3/4 cup softened margarine
1/2 cup firmly packed brown sugar
6 Tbsp. buttermilk
1 1/2 cups mashed ripe banana
3 eggs
1 1/2 tsp. vanilla extract
1 cup pecans
6 Tbsp. flour
1 pkg. (3-oz.) instant banana flavored pudding

Sift together cake flour, baking powder, soda, salt and sugar. Add shortening, brown sugar, buttermilk and bananas. Mix to dampen flour. Beat 2 minutes. Add eggs and vanilla and beat 1 minute longer. Fold in nuts. Spread into greased and paper-lined 9" layer-cake pans. Bake 375°F. 30 minutes. Prepare pudding according to

From Freezer to Sack

package instructions. Spread between cooled layers. Cut into wedges, wrap individually, label and freeze. Keeps up to 6 months.

BRAN AND DATE MUFFINS

2 cups boiling water
5 tsp. baking soda
1 cup shortening
2 cups granulated sugar
4 eggs, beaten
5 cups flour
½ Tbsp. salt
4 cups 100% bran cereal
2 cups 40% bran cereal
1 cup nuts
1 qt. buttermilk
2 cups dates, chopped

Pour boiling water over dates and soda. Cool. Cream shortening and sugar. Add remaining ingredients. Bake in greased paper-lined muffin tins at 400°F. for 20 minutes. Cool. Wrap each muffin tightly in wrap; label and freeze. Keeps up to 5 months.

CHEESECAKE

1½ cups vanilla wafer crumbs
⅓ cup melted margarine
2 Tbsp. granulated sugar
1 pkg. (8-oz.) cream cheese
⅔ cup sweetened condensed milk
1 tsp. grated lemon peel
3 Tbsp. lemon juice
1 cup whipped topping

Mix crumbs with margarine and sugar. Press into bottom and sides of 9" pie plate. Chill. Soften cheese at room temperature. Stir in milk, peel and juice; blend well. Fold in whipped topping. Spoon into chilled pie shell. Freeze. Cut into wedges and place in individual wedge-shaped containers with tight fitting lids and seal lid seams with freezer tape. Return to freezer. Keeps up to 2 months.

From Freezer to Sack

CHOCOLATE COOKIES

1 2/3 cup flour
2 tsp. baking powder
1/4 tsp. salt
1/8 tsp. baking soda
1/2 cup margarine
1 cup packed brown sugar
2 eggs, separated
2 1-oz. sq. unsweetened chocolate, melted
1 tsp. vanilla extract
1/2 cup milk
1 cup finely chopped walnuts

Sift together flour, baking powder, salt, and baking soda. Cream margarine with brown sugar until fluffy. Beat in egg yolks, chocolate and vanilla. Alternately add sifted flour mixture and milk, Add nuts. Drop by teaspoonfuls 1" apart on greased cookie sheet. Bake 350°F. 10 to 12 minutes. Cool. Wrap several to a package and freeze. Keeps up to 6 months.

DATE AND NUT BRAN BREAD

2 cups chopped dates
3 cups boiling water
4 cups sifted flour
4 tsp. baking soda
1 tsp. cinnamon
1/2 tsp. nutmeg
1/4 tsp. cloves
1 tsp. salt
3 cups 100% bran cereal
2 cups chopped walnuts
4 cups packed brown sugar
6 Tbsp. melted margarine
2 eggs, slightly beaten

Combine dates with boiling water and cool. Sift flour with baking soda, cinnamon, nutmeg, cloves and salt. Mix in bran and nuts. Mix dates and water with brown sugar, margarine and eggs. Add to flour mixture and stir to moisten flour. Spoon into 2 9½" x 5½" greased loaf pans. Bake at 350°F. for 60 to 65 minutes. Cool 10 minutes before removing from rack. Cool loaves completely before slicing into serving-sized portions. Wrap separately in freezer or plastic wrap, label and freeze. Keeps up to 3 months.

FRUIT BREAD

3 cups flour
1/2 tsp. salt
1 1/2 Tbsp. baking powder
1 cup sugar
1 cup raisins
3/4 cup dried mixed candied fruit
1 cup chopped nuts
3 eggs, beaten
1 1/2 cups milk
1/3 cup melted margarine

Sift together flour, salt, baking powder, and sugar. Stir in raisins, fruits, and nuts. Combine eggs with milk and margarine. Add to flour mixture, stirring just to blend. Line 9 1/2" x 5 1/2" loaf pan with waxed paper and grease. Spoon batter into pan and let stand at room temperature 30 minutes. Bake 350°F. for 1 hour. Let stand in pan 10 minutes before removing from pan and peeling off paper. Cool completely. Slice with sharp knife and wrap each slice individually; label and freeze. Keeps up to 3 months.

HONEY DATE-NUT BARS

3 eggs
1 cup honey
2 tsps. grated lemon rind
¼ tsp. salt
1 cup flour
1 tsp. baking powder
2 cups chopped dates
1½ cups chopped pecans

Beat eggs until thick and lemon colored. Add honey, rind and salt; mix well. Combine flour with baking powder and add, along with dates and nuts, to egg mixture. Mix well. Grease a 13" x 9" x 2" baking pan and line bottom with waxed paper. Spoon batter into pan and bake in oven, preheated to 325°F., for 40 minutes. Let stand 10 minutes, then loosen around edges with small knife. Turn out on board and pull off paper; cool. Cut into bars; wrap, label and freeze. Keeps up to 6 months.

HONEY-RAISIN QUICK BREAD

2 Tbsp. softened margarine
⅓ cup honey
3 Tbsp. sugar
2 eggs
⅔ cup whole wheat flour
1 cup all-purpose flour
1½ tsp. baking powder
¼ tsp. salt
½ tsp. baking soda
½ cup sour milk
½ cup raisins
½ cup chopped pecans
2 tsp. grated lomon rind

Cover raisins with boiling water and drain. Set aside. Cream margarine, honey and sugar. Add eggs, one at a time. Add whole wheat flour. Mix well. Alternately add remaining dry ingredients, and milk, beating until blended. Fold in nuts and lemon rind, then pour into greased loaf pan. Bake at 325°F. for 50 minutes. Cool completely before slicing. Wrap each slice individually and freeze. Keeps up to 6 months.

From Freezer to Sack

LEMON POUND CAKE

4 eggs
1 pkg. (2-layer size) yellow cake mix
1 pkg. (3¾-oz.) lemon pudding mix
¾ cup water
⅓ cup cooking oil
2 cups confectioner's sugar
⅓ cup freshly squeezed lemon juice

Beat eggs until thick and lemon colored. Add cake mix, pudding mix, water, and oil; beat 10 minutes with electric mixer. Pour into ungreased tube pan with removable bottom. Bake at 350°F. for 50 minutes.

Remove sides of pan from hot cake. With fork, prick holes in top of cake.

In saucepan, combine sugar and lemon juice; bring to boiling. Drizzle over top of cake. Cool completely. Remove pan bottom. Cut cake into slices, wrap, label and freeze. Keeps up to 6 months.

MARASCHINO CAKE

1 small bottle Maraschino cherries
1 cup pecans
1 cup dates, pitted
1 cup sugar
1 cup butter
1 egg, slightly beaten
2 cups flour
1 tsp. baking soda
1 tsp. vanilla
¾ cup Maraschino cherry juice

Combine all ingredients and mix well. Line oblong pan with wax paper. Spoon in cake batter. Bake 325°F. for 65 minutes. Cool, slice and wrap individually. Label and freeze. Keeps up to 6 months.

NUTMEG CAKE

1/2 cup butter
1 1/3 cup sugar
3 eggs
2 cups flour
1 tsp. baking powder
1 tsp. baking soda
2 tsp. nutmeg
Dash salt
1 cup buttermilk
6 Tbsp. butter
1/4 cup cream
1 cup brown sugar
3/4 cup flaked coconut

Cream together 1/2 cup butter and sugar until light and fluffy. Add eggs, one at a time, beating well after each addition. Sift together flour, baking powder, soda, nutmeg and salt; add alternately to creamed mixture with buttermilk, beating well after each addition. Turn into greased and floured cake pans. Bake at 375°F. for 25 minutes. Meanwhile, combine 6 Tbsp. butter, cream and brown sugar in saucepan. Bring to boiling. Pour over warm cake layer; top with coconut and nuts. Cool. Turn cooled untopped cake layer onto platter. Top with other cake layer, topping side down. Cut into wedges, wrap and freeze. Keeps up to 4 months.

PEANUT BUTTER MUFFINS

2 cups sifted flour
1 Tbsp. baking powder
1/2 cup peanut butter
1 cup milk
2 eggs
1/2 cup sugar
1/2 tsp. salt

Salt together flour and baking powder. Mix together peanut butter, milk, eggs, sugar and salt. Pour over dry ingredients; mix to just moisten dry ingredients.

Fill paper-lined muffin pans 2/3 full. Bake at 400°F. for 15 to 20 minutes. Cool. Wrap, label and freeze. Keeps up to 6 months.

PECAN LOAF

2½ cups sifted flour
1½ tsp. baking powder
¾ tsp. baking soda
½ tsp. salt
3 Tbsp. melted butter
1 cup orange juice
3 Tbsp. grated orange peel
1 cup finely cut-up pitted dates
1½ cups sugar
2 eggs
1 cup chopped pecans

Sift flour together with baking powder, soda, and salt. Mix together butter, juice, peel, dates, sugar, eggs and pecans. Stir in flour mixture and mix thoroughly. Pour into well greased and floured 9½" x 5¼" loaf pan. Bake 350°F. for 1 hour and 15 minutes. Cool in pan 10 minutes. Remove from pan, slice, wrap and freeze. Keeps up to 6 months.

From Freezer to Sack

Chapter 3

Waist Watchers

Oh, oh. You've done it again, haven't you? Too many milk shakes — and those cheeseburgers. Even if the fast food places served double scoops of cottage cheese or carrot sticks or rye crisps, who'd be able to resist the tantalizing temptation of hot French fries—with catsup? The thing to do now is keep away.

Maybe things wouldn't have gotten so out of shape if that coffee cart hadn't rolled by so often with its load of pastries. That vending machine down the hallway handing out candy bars hadn't helped either. The bulges spreading out over your waist-band and your will power seems to have gone to the Philippines for the winter. Learn to say, "No, thank you."

Every time your mind thinks "diet" your stomach squirms. Could it be possible that it still remembers being doused with all that unsweetened grapefruit juice last year? Or was it the diet where you fed it all those chalky-flavored milk drinks?

Cutting back on calories (shhh, don't say 'diet') needn't be so unpleasant. Many tasty meals are low in calories. Wouldn't you prefer Boston Clam Chowder or Teriyaki Chicken over a ham and cheese sandwich? How about passing up the cheesecake for Chocolate Angel Food Cake or Fresh Peach Paradise? In fact, you could have a full course meal —entree, salad, dessert and beverage —

47   **Waist Watchers**

for under 300 calories (less calories than one avocado-Swiss sandwich). No, I'm not teasing! Take a peek at the following low-calorie recipes and tell your stomach to mellow out.

Waist Watchers

BEVERAGES

ANISE-CINNAMON TEA

¼ lb. black tea leaves
1 Tbsp. anise seed
1 stick cinnamon

Break cinnamon stick into tiny pieces and combine with tea and anise. Store in tightly covered container. To brew, steep 1 tsp. per cup of boiling water. Strain and pour, hot, into thermos. (No calories.)

APPLE-BEEF BROTH

1 can condensed beef broth
½ soup can apple juice
Ground cinnamon

Combine beef broth and apple juice in saucepan. Heat through then pour into thermos. Sprinkle cinnamon into thermos. (2 servings, 46 calories each)

CARROT-PINEAPPLE COCKTAIL

1 medium-sized carrot, peeled and sliced
½ cup unsweetened pineapple juice
1 slice lemon
3 ice cubes

Put all ingredients into blender and run until all ingredients are liquified. Pour into chilled thermos. (84 calories)

Waist Watchers

CHILLED TOMATO BOUILLON

1 cup boiling water
2 beef bouillon cubes
3 cups tomato juice
1/2 cup chopped green pepper
1 Tbsp. lemon juice
1 tsp. Worcestershire sauce
1 tsp. sugar
1/2 tsp. monosodium glutamate
1/8 tsp. powdered cloves
1/8 tsp. pepper
6 drops garlic juice

Add bouillon to boiling water; stir to dissolve. Pour into saucepan along with remaining ingredients; place over medium heat and bring to boil; cover and simmer 8 to 10 minutes. Strain. Cool; chill in refrigerator. Pour 1½ cups into chilled thermos. Remainder will keep refrigerated up to 1 week. (72 calories per 1½ cup serving)

CLAM JUICE STINGER

1 bottle (7½-oz.) clam juice
1 Tbsp. lemon juice
1 can (12-oz.) vegetable juice cocktail
2 dashes hot pepper sauce

Combine all ingredients. Chill thoroughly. (2 servings, 63 calories each)

DILLED BEEF BROTH

2 cans (10½-oz. each) condensed beef broth
1 cup water
1/2 Tbsp. horseradish
1/2 tsp. dill weed

Combine all ingredients in large saucepan; heat to simmering, stirring occasionally. Pour into thermos. (4 servings, 54 calories each)

LEMON-MINT TEA

¼ lb. black tea leaves
¼ cup dried mint leaves
3 Tbsp. dried lemon peel

Combine tea, mint and peel. Store tightly covered. To brew, steep 1 tsp. per cup of water. May be enjoyed hot or iced. (No calories)

MAIN COURSES

BOSTON CLAM CHOWDER

1/2 cup drained canned clams
1/4 cup clam liquid
1/2 cup chopped onion
1/4 cup diced carrots
1/2 cup water
Dash each salt, pepper and thyme
1 cup skim milk

Put clams and liquid into saucepan. Add onion, carrots, water and seasonings. Cook, covered, over low heat 25 minutes. Add clams and milk, stirring constantly to blend. Simmer, stirring, 5 minutes. Divide into three portions. Pour one portion into thermos. Remaining portions can be reheated over double-boiler and will keep up to 3 days. (61 calories per serving)

CHICKEN BORSH

1 can (16 1/2-oz.) diced beets, undrained
2 cans (10 1/2-oz. each) beef consomme
1 cup water
1 Tbsp. flour
1/4 tsp. pepper
1 cup diced cooked chicken
1/3 cup lemon juice

Combine undrained beets, consomme and water in large saucepan. Stir in small amount of borsh liquid into flour to make a paste, then stir flour mixture into liquid in saucepan; add pepper. Simmer, covered, over low heat for 12 minutes.

Remove from heat and stir in chicken and lemon juice. Pour 1/4 borsh into thermos. Remainder will keep up to 5 days. (145 calories per serving)

Waist Watchers

CHICKEN SALAD

3 cups cooked chicken breasts,
skinned and diced
1½ Tbsp. vinegar
½ tsp. paprika
¼ tsp. seasoned pepper
½ tsp. salt
¼ tsp. garlic powder
½ cup cottage cheese
1 Tbsp. buttermilk
¼ cup chopped onion
½ cup pared and chopped cucumber
1 Tbsp. chopped pimiento
8 radishes, halved
1 hard-cooked egg, riced
Butter lettuce

Combine vinegar, salt, paprika, pepper and garlic powder in bowl. Add chicken and toss lightly. Chill at least 1 hour.

Combine cottage cheese, buttermilk, onion and radishes in blender. Whirl until cottage cheese is smooth and radishes are chopped. Combine chicken, cucumber and pimento. Line 3 individual containers with lettuce. Spoon in salad mixture. Before packing container in lunch bag, pour ⅓ of the cottage cheese dressing over salad and garnish with riced egg. Unused servings keep 3 days. (215 calories per serving)

CHILLED PINEAPPLE-MEAT LOAF

3 pineapple slices, halved
1 lb. lean ground chuck
1/2 lb. ground veal
1 slice bread, finely crumbled
2/3 cup skim milk
1/2 cup chopped onion
1 egg, beaten
1/2 tsp. salt
1/2 tsp. monosodium glutamate
1/4 tsp. paprika
1/2 tsp. marjoram
1/8 tsp. thyme
1/8 tsp. pepper

Grease a 9½ x 5¼ x 2¾" loaf pan. Arrange pineapple slices in bottom of pan. Mix together remaining ingredients and pack mixture lightly into pan. Bake 350°F. 1½ hours. Pour off excess juices from loaf, loosen meat gently from sides and invert onto platter. Cool. Slice loaf into eight slices. Wrap and slice individually. Extra portions may be frozen for later use. (184 calories per serving)

CUCUMBER-CHIVE SOUP

1 medium-sized cucumber, shredded
1 1/4 cups skim milk
1 Tbsp. flour
1/4 tsp. salt
1/4 tsp. paprika
Dash pepper
1 bouillon cube
2 Tbsp. chopped chives

Pour milk into top of double boiler. Sprinkle flour, salt, paprika and pepper over milk. Beat with electric mixer until blended. Add cucumber, bouillon and chives. Cook over simmering water, stirring constantly, 15 to 20 minutes or until mixture thickens slightly. Cool; chill in refrigerator. Spoon 1/3 into chilled thermos. Remaining portions should be used within 3 days. (77 calories per serving)

Waist Watchers

HAMBURGER-VEGETABLE SOUP

4½ cups water
6 beef bouillon cubes
1 can (16-oz.) stewed tomatoes
2 cups diced celery
1 carrot, diced
2 garlic cloves, minced
2 bay leaves
½ tsp. pepper
½ lb. lean ground round steak
1 pkg. (10-oz.) frozen peas

Combine water and bouillon cubes in saucepan, bring to boiling. Brown meat in skillet, breaking into pieces with fork; add to bouillon along with remaining ingredients. Cover and simmer 15 minutes. Remove bay leaves. Pour serving portions into a wide mouth thermos, cool and refrigerate remainder. Keeps up to 5 days. (6 servings, 130 calories each)

HERRING SALAD

1 jar (8-oz.) pickled herring in wine sauce
1 Tbsp. skimmed milk
½ tsp. lemon juice
1 container (8-oz.) cottage cheese
½ cup sliced onion, separated into rings
Watercress

Drain herring and set aside. Combine milk, lemon juice and cottage cheese in blender; whirl at low speed to form smooth sauce. Line 4 individual serving containers with watercress. Spoon in herring and onion. Top with cottage cheese sauce just before packing container in lunch bag. Unused portions keep up to 5 days. (165 calories per serving)

HONEY-ORANGE CHICKEN

4 chicken breasts, skinned
1/2 tsp. salt
1/4 tsp. pepper
1/4 cup fresh orange juice
2 Tbsp. honey
1 tsp. Worcestershire sauce
1/4 tsp. dry mustard

Place chicken in shallow baking pan, sprinkle with salt and pepper. Bake 375°F. 30 minutes. Combine remaining ingredients and brush over chicken frequently as it continues baking 30 minutes longer. Cool. Wrap each piece in aluminum foil and chill until used. Keeps up to 5 days. (4 servings, 200 calories per serving)

JELLIED VEAL LOAF

1 3/4 cups beef broth
1/2 cup chopped onion
1/2 tsp. celery seed
4 peppercorns
1 Tbsp. low-calorie lemon-flavored gelatin
1 Tbsp. prepared horseradish
1 tsp. salt
2 cups finely ground cooked veal
1/3 cup finely chopped parsley

Combine broth, onion, celery seed and peppercorns in saucepan and simmer over low heat 8 to 10 minutes. Strain broth, discarding solids. Put gelatin into bowl and pour hot liquid over, stirring until gelatin is dissolved. Stir in horseradish and salt. Chill until gelatin mixture begins to set. Lightly oil loaf pan. Fold veal and parsley into the thickened gelatin mixture and chill until firmly set. Unmold on platter; slice into 8 sections, wrapping each separately. Portions will freeze or keep, refrigerated, up to 6 days. To pack in lunch, line container with lettuce, add a slice of loaf and cover with a tight fitting lid. (109 calories per serving)

Waist Watchers

PICKLED SHRIMP

1 lb. fresh shrimp in shells
1/4 cup celery leaves
2 1/4 Tbsp. pickling spice
1 tsp. salt
2/3 cup sliced onion
4 bay leaves
2/3 cup low-calorie Italian salad dressing
1/2 cup white vinegar
1 Tbsp. undrained capers
1 1/2 tsp. celery seed
Dash hot pepper sauce

Place shrimp, celery leaves, pickling spice and salt in saucepan; cover with boiling water. Simmer, covered, 5 minutes. Drain; cool; then peel and devein shrimp. Place shrimp, onion and bay leaves in shallow dish. Combine remaining ingredients and pour over shrimp mixture. Cover and marinate at least 24 hours.

Line paper bowl with lettuce leaves; top with 5 drained shrimp and a few onion rings. Seal bowl with plastic wrap. Remaining shrimp will keep in marinate up to 1 week. (115 calories per serving)

SHRIMP SALAD

1/2 cup low-calorie French dressing
1/2 cup yogurt
3 Tbsp. lemon juice
6 cups finely shredded cabbage
2 cans (4 1/2-oz.) shrimp, drained
1/2 cup snipped parsley
5 green onions, chopped
1/2 cup sliced ripe olives

Combine dressing, yogurt and lemon juice, stir with fork to blend. Add remaining ingredients and toss well. Spoon into 4 individual containers, cover and chill. Keeps up to 5 days. (200 calories per serving)

SLOPPY JOES

1/2 medium-sized onion, chopped
1/2 cup chopped celery
1/2 lb. lean ground chuck
1/2 cup tomato puree
1/4 cup catsup
1 cup canned tomatoes
1/4 tsp. hickory-smoked salt
Dash cayenne
Hamburger buns

Combine onion, celery and meat in skillet. Slowly cook over medium heat until meat is browned. Add puree, catsup, tomatoes, salt and cayenne pepper. Simmer, uncovered, for 30 minutes. For each serving, spoon 1/3 cup meat sauce into small thermos. Place 1/2 hamburger bun in a paper plate and wrap with plastic wrap. When ready to serve, spoon sauce over bun. Unused mixture may be divided into serving portions and frozen, or stored in the refrigerator for up to 6 days. (165 calories per serving)

TERIYAKI CHICKEN

4 chicken breasts, skinned
1/2 cup lemon juice
1/4 cup water
3 Tbsp. soy sauce
1/4 tsp. ground ginger
1/2 tsp. garlic salt

Combine juice, water, soy sauce, ginger and salt. Pour over raw chicken breasts and marinate overnight. Remove chicken from marinade and broil in oven 20 to 25 minutes, turning and basting quently. Cool. Wrap each piece in aluminum foil and refrigerate. Keeps up to 5 days, or can be frozen and kept up to 3 months. (4 servings, 160 calories each)

Waist Watchers

TOMATOES STUFFED WITH CRAB

2 medium to large tomatoes
²/₃ cup crab meat
¼ cup low-calorie Russian dressing
1 Tbsp. celery
1 Tbsp. capers
2 tsp. lemon juice
¼ tsp. salt
¼ tsp. pepper

Remove pulp from tomato shells and combine with remaining ingredients. Chill tomato shells and filling separately. Spoon filling into shells, wrap in plastic wrap and place in paper bowls. Tomatoes will keep up to 3 days. (2 servings, 103 calories each)

TUNA BALLS

1 can (7-oz.) water-pack tuna, drained
1 pkg. (3-oz.) Neufchatel cheese, softened
2 Tbsp. finely chopped celery
1 Tbsp. freshly squeezed lemon juice
½ tsp. Worcestershire sauce
Dash salt

Blend tuna and cheese. Add remaining ingredients and mix well. Form into 30 small balls. Chill well; then spear with tooth picks. Place 10 in lettuce-lined paper bowl. Cover with plastic wrap. Remainder keeps up to 6 days. (160 calories per serving)

SIDE DISHES

APPLE SLAW

1 1/2 cups shredded cabbage
1 medium-sized apple, diced
2 Tbsp. evaporated milk
1 Tbsp. lemon juice
1 tsp. grated onion
1 Tbsp. sugar
1/2 Tbsp. celery seed
1/2 tsp. salt
1/8 tsp. pepper

Toss together cabbage and apple. Combine remaining ingredients and mix well. Pour over cabbage mixture. Spoon equal amounts into 3 individual serving containers. Chill. Keeps up to 4 days. (61 calories per serving)

BEAN AND BEET SALAD

1/4 cup vinegar
1 Tbsp. mayonnaise
1 Tbsp. grated onion
1/4 tsp. salt
Dash hot pepper sauce
1 can (16-oz.) cut green beans, drained
1 can (16-oz.) diced beets, drained

Combine first 5 ingredients and mix well. Add vegetables and toss. Divide into 6 individual containers. Cover and chill. Salad keeps up to 1 week. (55 calories per serving)

Waist Watchers

MARINATED MUSHROOMS

1 cup tarragon vinegar
2 Tbsp. salad oil
2 small garlic cloves, crushed
2 bay leaves
½ tsp. dried thyme leaves
½ lb. small fresh mushrooms
3 cups water

Combine vinegar, oil, garlic, bay and thyme; mix well. Place mushrooms in saucepan and add water. Bring to boil over medium-high heat and simmer 5 minutes. Drain well. Cool. Pour marinade over mushrooms, cover and refrigerate overnight. Drain. Divide mushrooms into 5 individual containers; cover and chill until used. Keeps up to 1 week. (30 calories per serving)

VEGETABLE SLAW

¼ cup cider vinegar
1½ Tbsp. minced parsley
½ tsp. dry mustard
Dash salt and pepper
3 cups shredded cabbage
2 cups shredded carrots
2 cups canned green beans, drained
1 cup diced green pepper
¼ cup minced onion

Mix all ingredients in bowl and toss lightly. Spoon into individual serving containers. Remainder keeps up to 5 days. (80 calories per 1 cup serving)

DESSERTS

APRICOT WHIP

¾ cup dried apricots
1 cup boiling water
1 tsp. sweetening solution
2 egg whites
Dash salt

Pour boiling water over apricots, cover and soak 1 to 2 hours; then simmer over medium heat 30 minutes. Cool; pour into blender and puree. Blend in sweetener. Beat egg whites with salt until peaks are formed; gradually add puree and continue beating until mixture is uniform in color. Spoon into 4 individual containers, cover and chill. Keeps up to 1 week. (81 calories per serving)

CHOCOLATE ANGEL FOOD CAKE

12 egg whites, room temperature
⅔ cup sifted cake flour
½ cup sugar
⅓ cup cocoa
½ tsp. salt
1½ tsp. cream of tartar
¾ cup sugar
1½ tsp. vanilla extract

Sift together flour and ½ cup sugar and cocoa. Set aside. Add salt to egg whites and beat with electric mixer until frothy. Beat in cream of tartar until peaks are formed. Sprinkle ¾ cup sugar evenly over surface and carefully fold into whites. Blend in vanilla. Sift 4 Tbsp. of flour mixture over egg-white mixture and fold gently together. Repeat procedure until all the flour mixture has been folded in.

Carefully spoon batter into 10" tubed pan. Cut through batter with knife to break large air bubbles. Bake 350°F. 45 to 50 minutes.

Immediately invert pan on cooling rack; allow to cool completely. Cut into 14 sections. Wrap each piece individually. May be frozen for later use. (108 calories per serving)

Waist Watchers

EGG CUSTARD

1 cup skim milk
1 egg, slightly beaten
4 non-caloric sweetening tablets
Dash salt
1 tsp. vanilla extract

Scald milk in top of double boiler. Blend in sweetening tablets. Stirring constantly, gradually add scalded milk to egg mixture. Return to cleaned double boiler top. Cook over simmering water, stirring constantly and rapidly, until mixture coats spoon. Remove and cool to lukewarm over cold water. Blend in vanilla. Spoon into 3 small jars or containers with tight fitting lids. Chill. Keeps up to 4 days. (55 calories per serving)

FRESH PEACH PARADISE

4 ripe peaches
4 oz. plain yogurt
1 Tbsp. honey

Peel and slice peaches into bowl. Combine yogurt and honey, mix well, then fold into fruit. Pack in 2 individual serving containers. Chill. Keeps up to 3 days. (90 calories per serving)

FRUIT SOUP

3 Tbsp. quick-cooking tapioca
2 Tbsp. sugar
¼ tsp. salt
1 can (6-oz.) orange juice concentrate
2 peaches, sliced
1 banana, sliced
1 orange, peeled and sectioned
½ cup sliced strawberries
1½ Tbsp. lemon juice

Over high heat, cook tapioca, sugar, salt and 1 cup boiling water, stirring occasionally until mixture comes to a boil. Remove from heat. Add to tapioca mixture 1½ cups water and orange juice concentrate. Cool 15 minutes. Add remaining ingredients, stir, then divide into 6 individual serving containers. Chill. Keeps up to 1 week. (100 calories per serving)

LIME-FRUIT GELATIN

1 envelope unflavored gelatin
1 can (16-oz.) fruit cocktail, drained and rinsed
¼ cup lime juice
2 Tbsp. sugar
¼ cup non-fat dry milk powder

Pour ¼ cup water into saucepan and sprinkle gelatin over top. Cook, stirring, over medium heat until gelatin is dissolved. Pour gelatin into medium bowl and add fruit, 3 Tbsp. lime juice, sugar and 1 cup water. Chill 45 minutes.

Place dry milk, 1 Tbsp. lime juice and ¼ cup ice water in a medium-sized bowl. With mixer, beat at high speed until stiff peaks form. Gently fold whipped milk into gelatin mixture. Pour into square 8" x 8" pan and chill. Cut into 8 squares. To serve, line individual containers with lettuce, then add square of gelatin. Unused portions keep up to 6 days. (45 calories per serving)

Waist Watchers

MAPLE CUSTARD

2 cups skimmed milk
¼ cup sugar
2 eggs
2 tsp. maple extract
Dash salt
¼ tsp. cinnamon
Dash nutmeg

Combine all ingredients in medium bowl and beat well with wire whisk or fork. Pour into six 6-oz. custard cups; place in metal baking pan filled with 1" hot water. Bake in preheated 350°F. oven for 50 to 60 minutes. Chill. Keeps up to 5 days. (90 calories per serving)

PEACH-TAPIOCA PUDDING

4 peaches, peeled and sliced
1 egg yolk, slightly beaten
1½ cups skim milk
3 Tbsp. quick-cooking tapioca
1 tsp. non-caloric sweetening solution
Dash salt
1 egg white
½ tsp. vanilla extract
½ tsp. almong extract

Combine egg yolk, milk, tapioca, sweetener and salt. Set over medium heat and bring mixture to a full boil, stirring constantly. Remove from heat. Beat egg white until peaks form, then gradually add to tapioca. Blend in vanilla and almond extracts. In 4 individual serving containers, alternate tapioca and sliced peaches. Chill. Keeps up to 4 days. (84 calories per serving)

Chapter 4

Likable Leftovers

Disagreeable occurrences which befall many potentially flavorful leftovers are that they ripen in their containers in obscure corners of the refrigerator. Remembering what happens then? Right! A questionable mass ringed with bluish-green mold. Even the garbage disposal could gag on that.

So, what's likable about a leftover? For one thing, you don't have to start from scratch to make one.

To concoct the dish is the difficult part; eating it is easy. Why, then, do so many individuals have difficulty consuming the remnants of a meal? Some people don't like repetition, i.e., hot fried chicken for supper, cold fried chicken for lunch. Others have difficulties working leftovers into their ensuing menus. These are simple problems to solve.

During meal planning, for instance, schedule a nice juicy roast beef for supper. The following morning use the remainder to prepare Beef-Potato Hash (no repitition here), Meat 'N Potatoes in Peppers (good way to use extra cooked potatoes), or a thick Roast Beef Sandwich.

Some of you may be snickering about the roast beef. I can't remember the last time I had any, either. Having leftover chicken or turkey is far more probable. The roasted turkey you had for supper can become Curried Turkey Salad or a Turkey Pocket Sandwich. That unconsumed

67   **Likable Leftovers**

chicken breast or thigh (if you're lucky enough to have one) makes delicious Chicken Stuffed Eggs or Marinated Chicken Salad.

Don't overlook leftover cooked rice — great in rice pudding or fried rice. Leftover vegetables are super added to soup stock, stew or fritters. The birds don't need the bread crumbs and dried heels; use them in stuffing, bread pudding, or coating for breaded chicken.

The main point is to use up any excess cooked food as soon as possible. Don't view an uneaten tidbit as something which will decay into a slimmy mess, then startle you when you clean the refrigerator. Treat such leftovers as dividends and put them to work stretching your lunch budget.

Likable Leftovers   **68**

HOT MAIN DISHES

BEEF-POTATO HASH

3 cups cooked, diced beef
4 cups cooked, diced potatoes
1 medium onion, minced
¼ cup margarine
1 cup cooked green beans, carrots, peas, or corn
1 cup leftover gravy
Salt and pepper

Brown beef, potatoes and onion in margarine. Add vegetables, gravy, and salt and pepper. Heat thoroughly. Spoon desired portion into a wide mouthed thermos. Unused portion may be reheated and will keep refrigerated up to 4 days. (4 servings)

CHICKEN A LA KING

1½ cups milk
2 Tbsp. margarine
2 Tbsp. flour
1 cup cold cooked chicken, diced
½ cup canned mushrooms, sliced
1 egg yolk, slightly beaten
¼ cup pimiento, chopped
1 Tbsp. green pepper
Salt, pepper, and paprika to taste
2 patty shells

Melt 2 Tbsp. margarine in skillet; stir in flour. Add milk slowly, stirring constantly. Cook until thickened. Add remaining ingredients, heat, then spoon into a wide mouthed thermos. Wrap patty shells separately.

To serve, place shells in paper bowl and spoon a la King over top. (serves 1 to 2)

Likable Leftovers

FISH SOUP

3/4 cup boned cooked fish
1 pt. milk
Dash mace
3 Tbsp. margarine
1 1/2 Tbsp. flour
1/2 tsp. salt
1/4 tsp. pepper

Rub fish through sieve. Scald milk. Add onion, mace and fish. Melt 1 1/2 Tbsp. margarine in skillet; add flour, then stir into milk mixture. Cook over medium low heat until thickened. Stir remaining margarine, salt and pepper into soup. Pour into thermos. (serves 1 to 2)

FISH STEW

2 cups cooked, flaked fish
3 medium-sized potatoes
4 cups water
2 cups finely diced cooked carrots
1 cup frozen green peas
1 medium-sized onion, minced
3 Tbsp. margarine
3 Tbsp. flour
2 cups milk
2 egg yolks, well beaten
Salt and pepper to taste

Cook potatoes in water until well done. Mash potatoes in cooking liquid. Melt margarine in saucepan and gradually add flour; slowly stir into potato liquid. Cook over medium heat, stirring, until smooth. Add remaining ingredients and heat thoroughly. Pour desired amount into thermos. Remainder can be refrigerated and reheated at a later date. Keeps up to 3 days. (serves 4)

SALMON CHOWDER

(A quick and delicious way to use up bits of leftover cooked potatoes, rice, beans, corn, carrots, etc.)

1 can salmon
1 qt. milk
2 Tbsp. minced onion
2 Tbsp. margarine
2 Tbsp. flour
½ cup cooked diced potatoes or leftover rice
1 cup cooked vegetables
Salt and pepper to taste

Combine salmon with milk and onion; heat in top part of double boiler over simmering water 20 minutes. Rub together flour and margarine; stir into chowder and cook until thickened. Add potatoes or rice and vegetables. Season to taste. Pour desired amount into thermos. Remainder may be cooled and refrigerated, then reheated and used within 3 days. (serves 4)

GREEN PEA SOUP WITH HAM

1 pkg. (12-oz.) frozen peas
2 cups milk
1 Tbsp. flour
2 Tbsp. margarine
¼ tsp. salt
¼ tsp. nutmeg
1/8 tsp. pepper
½ cup chopped onion
1 cup cooked diced ham

Put 1 cup milk, flour, margarine, salt, nutmeg, pepper, and onion in blender container. Cover and blend smooth. Add peas and remaining milk; puree.

Pour blended mixture into saucepan; add ham. Bring to a boil, remove from heat and pour into a thermos. (serves 1)

Likable Leftovers

HAM BALLS IN CRANBERRY SAUCE

1 1/2 cups cubed cooked ham
1 1/2 slices of bread, crumbled
1 egg, beaten
2 Tbsp. milk
1 Tbsp. salad oil
2/3 cup jellied cranberry sauce
1/2 Tbsp. steak sauce
1 tsp. brown sugar
1/2 tsp. salad oil
1/2 tsp. prepared mustard

Place 1/2 cup ham in blender container; blend until coarsely chopped. Set aside. Repeat with remaining ham. Combine ham with bread, egg, and milk; shape into 8 to 10 balls. Brown balls in 1 Tbsp. hot oil. Drain, place remaining ingredients in blender container; blend smooth. Pour over balls. Cover, cook 20 minutes, then spoon into wide mouthed thermos. (serves 3)

HAM AND SPLIT PEA SOUP

1 cup dried split peas
2 1/2 qts. cold water
1 ham bone
1/2 cup chopped onion
1 pt. milk
3 Tbsp. margarine
2 Tbsp. flour
1/2 tsp. pepper

Soak peas in water to cover for several hours; drain and add cold water, ham bone and onion. Simmer three or four hours, or until soft. Discard bone and cool soup. Puree in blender or rub through sieve. Melt margarine, add flour, and salt and pepper. Stir into pureed soup. Reheat desired portion and pour into thermos. If too thick, soup may be diluted with a little milk. Remainder keeps up to 7 days refrigerated or up to 6 months frozen. (makes 6 servings)

CREAMED TURKEY

1 chicken bouillon cube
1 cup mushroom liquid (add water to make complete cup)
1 cup milk
¼ cup margarine
¼ cup flour
¼ tsp. salt
½ tsp. paprika
1 tsp. grated onion
1½ cups diced cooked turkey
1 can (4-oz.) mushrooms, drained
¼ cup ripe olives

Dissolve bouillon in mushroom liquid and water over medium heat. Add milk. Melt margarine in saucepan; add flour and stir over low heat until thickened. Add remaining ingredients. Heat; spoon into wide mouthed thermos. Serve over corn bread or chow mein noodles which had been placed in a paper bowl and securely wrapped in plastic wrap. (serves 2)

TURKEY ROYAL

1 cup diced, cooked turkey
¼ cup cooked peas or green beans
1 can (4-oz.) mushrooms
2 Tbsp. pimento strips
½ Tbsp. minced parsley
½ Tbsp. minced chives
1 Tbsp. minced onion
2 Tbsp. margarine
3 Tbsp. flour
½ tsp. salt
2 egg yolks
1 cup sour cream

Saute pimento, parsley, chives and onion in margarine. Blend in flour, then gradually add milk, stirring constantly until mixture thickens. Vigorously stir 3 Tbsp. hot mixture into egg yolks, then stir into cream sauce. With wire whip, beat in sour cream. Add peas or beans, mushrooms, and turkey. Heat thoroughly.

Spoon into a wide mouthed thermos. Serve over potato or dinner rolls. Remainder may be kept refrigerated for up to 5 days. (serves 2)

73   **Likable Leftovers**

COLD MAIN DISHES

CORNED BEEF-POTATO SALAD

(This tangy main dish salad makes good use of leftover boiled potatoes and corned beef.)

> **2 cups cubed, cooked potatoes, peeled**
> **1 cup cubed, cooked corned beef**
> **¼ cup chopped sweet pickle**
> **¼ cup chopped celery**
> **¼ cup chopped onion**
> **2 Tbsp. salad oil**
> **1 Tbsp. wine vinegar**
> **¼ tsp. salt**
> **¼ tsp. garlic powder**
> **¼ tsp. pepper**
> **⅓ cup sour cream**
> **1 tsp. horseradish**

Combine potatoes, meat, pickles, celery, and onion. Toss lightly. Place remaining ingredients in jar and shake until well mixed. Pour over salad. Cover bowl and chill at least 2 hours. Spoon into 2 individual serving containers. (serves 2)

Likable Leftovers

MEAT 'N POTATOES IN PEPPERS

Instant mashed potato buds
(or 2½ cups leftover mashed potatoes)
1 cup cubed, cooked roast beef
1 hard-cooked egg, chopped
¼ cup pickle relish
1 Tbsp. minced onion
1 Tbsp. chopped pimento
2 Tbsp. vinegar
4 small green peppers

Prepare potatoes as directed on package for 4 servings. Stir in meat, eggs, relish, onion, pimento and vinegar; chill.

Cut thin slices from top of green peppers. Remove seeds and membranes. Spoon salad into shells. Chill until ready to pack in lunch bag. Mound filling into shells and wrap with plastic wrap. (serves 4)

ROAST BEEF SALAD

2 cups diced, cooked roast beef
1 cup diced, cooked potatoes, carrots, peas,
green beans and/or beets
½ cup mayonnaise
2 hard-cooked eggs, diced
1 medium onion, minced
½ cup chopped sweet pickles
Salt and pepper to taste

Combine ingredients and toss well. Chill thoroughly. Keeps up to 5 days. (serves 2)

CHICKEN AND CREAM CHEESE SANDWICH FILLING

1 pkg. (3-oz.) cream cheese
1 Tbsp. milk
1 cup diced, cooked chicken
1/3 cup minced onion
Salt and pepper to taste

Soften cream cheese with milk. Combine with remaining ingredients and mix well. Makes 5 sandwiches. (Good filling for freezer sandwiches.)

CHICKEN SALAD BUNS

1/3 cup mayonnaise
1/2 tsp. salt
1 tsp. vinegar
1/4 tsp. celery seed
Dash pepper
2 cups diced, cooked chicken
1 cup chopped celery
2 Tbsp. chopped dill pickle
1/4 cup slivered almonds
2 tsp. grated onions
5 hard-crusted sandwich rolls
Butter or margarine

Combine all ingredients except rolls and butter. Butter split rolls and spread with filling. Keeps up to 4 days. (serves 4)

CHICKEN SALAD ORIENTAL

1 1/2 cups diced, cooked chicken
2/3 cup drained pineapple tidbits
1/2 cup fresh mung bean sprouts
1 can (5-oz.) water chestnuts, sliced
1 Tbsp. sliced green onion
1/3 cup dairy sour cream
1/2 tsp. ground ginger

Combine chicken with remaining ingredients and mix well. Spoon into lettuce lined containers with tight fitting lids. Keeps up to 3 days. (serves 2)

Likable Leftovers

CHICKEN STUFFED EGGS

4 hard-cooked eggs
1/2 cup cooked chicken, minced
1 Tbsp. mayonnaise
Dash salt, pepper, garlic powder, and paprika
1 tsp. minced chives
Watercress
Bottled Russian dressing

Halve eggs lengthwise; mash yolks and combine with chicken, mayonnaise, seasonings, and chives. Carefully pack yolk mixture into egg whites. Line 2 individual serving containers with watercress and nestle 4 egg halves in each. Top with a spoonful of dressing and cover with a tight fitting lid. Salad keeps up to 3 days. (serves 2)

COLD CURRIED CHICKEN SOUP

1 tart apple, pared, cored and sliced
1/4 cup onion
1 Tbsp. margarine
1 tsp. curry powder
Dash salt and pepper
2 drops hot pepper sauce
1 cup chicken broth
1/4 cup cooking sherry
1/4 cup light cream
1/4 cup finely diced, cooked chicken

Saute apple and onion in margarine over low heat until soft. Stir in curry, salt, pepper, hot pepper sauce, broth, and wine. Simmer, covered, 10 minutes, stirring often. Cool 15 minutes, then puree in blender. Chill. Before pouring into chilled thermos, stir in chicken and cream. (serves 1)

MARINATED CHICKEN SALAD

1 Tbsp. white wine vinegar
3 Tbsp. vegetable oil
1/2 tsp. salt
1/4 tsp. pepper
1/4 tsp. crushed tarragon leaves
1 cup cubed, cooked chicken
1/2 cup thinly sliced, fresh mushrooms
1/4 cup diced green pepper
1 medium tomato, cut in wedges
1/2 cup diced, peeled cucumber
Lettuce

Combine first 5 ingredients. Add next 3 ingredients and toss lightly. Cover tightly and marinate in refrigerator overnight. Add tomatoes and cucumber. Pile in lettuce lined paper bowls. Wrap securely with plastic wrap. (serves 2)

HAM LOAF SANDWICH

2 cups, chopped, cooked ham
1/2 cup dry bread crumbs
1/2 cup finely diced onion
3 Tbsp. minced pimento
2 Tbsp. minced green pepper
1/3 cup tomato soup
2 eggs, slightly beaten

Combine all ingredients and mix thoroughly. Shape in loaf pan and bake 350°F. 40 minutes. Cool, then chill. Slice and sandwich desired amount between 2 slices of buttered bread (also good with a dab of horseradish). Remaining loaf may be wrapped and frozen or kept in the refrigerator for up to 5 days.

Likable Leftovers

HAM-MACARONI SALAD

2 cups macaroni
2 Tbsp. salad oil
2 Tbsp. vinegar
1 Tbsp. minced onion
1/4 tsp. seasoned salt
1/4 tsp. pepper
1 cup diced cheddar cheese
2/3 cup mayonnaise
1 can (17-oz.) peas, drained
1 cup ham
1 cup diced celery

Cook macaroni; drain. While hot, drizzle with oil and vinegar. Add onion, seasonings, and cheese; toss well. Gently mix in peas, ham, celery, and mayonnaise. Chill thoroughly. Pack in lettuce lined containers with tight fitting lids. Keeps up to 5 days. (serves 4)

HAM MOUSSE

(A rich main course made from leftover bits of ham.)

1 cup chopped, cooked ham
1 1/2 Tbsp. margarine
1 1/2 Tbsp. flour
1 cup light cream
Dash salt and pepper
1/8 tsp. paprika
1/2 Tbsp. gelatin
1 Tbsp. cold milk
1/2 cup whipping cream

Make white sauce by cooking margarine and flour to a paste; slowly stir in light cream and seasonings. Soften gelatin in cold milk for 5 minutes, then add to white sauce and simmer until gelatin is dissolved. Add ham; set aside and cool. Whip cream. Just before mixture begins to stiffen, fold in whipped cream. Pour into 3 individual containers and chill until set. Cover each with plastic wrap or foil. Mousse will keep up to 4 days. (serves 3)

Likable Leftovers

HAM AND RICE SALAD

2 cups cooked rice
1/2 tsp. salt
1 cup mayonnaise
1/4 tsp. pepper
2 Tbsp. lemon juice
2 tsp. grated onion
2 tsp. prepared mustard
3 cups diced, cooked ham
2 cups pineapple cubes
2 cups diced celery

Combine mayonnaise, salt, pepper, lemon juice, onion, and mustard. Mix well, then chill. Combine rice, ham, pineapple and celery. Add dressing. Chill. Spoon into covered containers. Remainder will keep up to 4 days. (serves 6)

EAST INDIAN LAMB SALAD

(A quick main dish with an exotic flair.)

1 cup cooked, diced lamb
1/4 cup shredded coconut
1/2 cup thinly sliced celery
1 medium-sized orange, peeled and sectioned
1/2 cup mayonnaise
2 Tbsp. wine vinegar
1/2 tsp. salt
1 tsp. curry powder
1/4 tsp. pepper

In bowl, combine lamb, coconut, celery, and orange. Mix together mayonnaise, vinegar, salt, curry and pepper; pour over lamb mixture and toss well. Spoon into two lettuce lined containers with tight fitting lids. Chill. Unused portion will keep up to 4 days. (serves 2)

Likable Leftovers

LAMB AND CHEESE SANDWICHES

4 slices whole grain bread
2 Tbsp. margarine
2 thick slices cooked lamb
1 Tbsp. chili sauce
¼ cup sliced sweet pickles
2 slices Swiss cheese

Spread bread with mayonnaise. Top 2 with lamb, chili sauce, pickles, and cheese. Top with remaining 2 slices of bread.

LAMB LOAF

¼ cup dry bread crumbs
3 cups ground lean cooked lamb
½ cup finely ground lean ham
1 cup finely chopped onion
3 tomatoes, peeled, seeded, and chopped
1 Tbsp. chopped mint
2 sprigs chopped fresh rosemary (optional)
2 eggs, slightly beaten

Grease loaf pan well and coat with some of the crumbs. Combine lamb, ham, onion, tomatoes, herbs, and seasonings. Add remaining bread crumbs, mix well and bind with eggs. Cover and bake 35 minutes. Cool. Chill. Slice into serving-sized slices and wrap in plastic wrap for lunches. May also be frozen.

LAMB LUNCHEON PLATTER

¼ lb. cooked, sliced lamb
4 oz. sliced Muenster cheese
2 deviled eggs
6 radish roses
8 ripe olives
1 tomato, sliced
½ Tbsp. mayonnaise
1½ Tbsp. vinegar
1 Tbsp. catsup
¼ tsp. salt
¼ tsp. margarine

Divide lamb, cheese, eggs, radishes, olives, and tomatoes into 2 equal portions. Place each portion of lamb, cheese, and eggs in a sandwich bag. Radishes, tomatoes, and olives are packed in separate bags. Combine mayonnaise, vinegar, catsup, salt and margoram. Mix well. Divide into two small containers with tight fitting lids.

Pack one bag of meat, cheese, and eggs along with a bag of olives, tomatoes, and radishes in lunch sack. Include a fork, folded paper plate, and container of herb dressing. To serve, arrange meat, egg, and vegetables on paper plate; top with dressing. Unused serving will keep up to 3 days. (serves 2)

LAMB AND ONION SANDWICHES

½ tsp. dried mint leaves
½ Tbsp. chopped parsley
¼ tsp. thyme
¼ tsp. salt
Dash pepper
2 Tbsp. vinegar
¼ cup olive oil
2 sweet Spanish onions, sliced
3 thick slices cooked lamb
6 slices rye bread, buttered

Combine, mint, parsley, thyme, salt, pepper, vinegar, and oil. Place onions in shallow dish; pour dressing over and allow onions to marinate overnight. Arrange onions on three slices of bread, top with lamb and remaining slices of bread.

83 **Likable Leftovers**

MEDITERRANEAN VEAL SALAD

1 1/2 cups leftover veal roast,
  cut into thin strips
1/4 cup bottled herb-and-garlic
  French style dressing
3 medium cold boiled potatoes, sliced
1/2 cup celery, finely chopped
2 Tbsp. minced onion
1/4 cup mayonnaise
2 Tbsp. pimentos, diced
1/4 cup sliced olives
1/4 cup minced parsley

Combine all ingredients in large bowl. Chill thoroughly. Pack lightly in plastic containers lined with lettuce; fit with tight fitting lid. (2 generous servings)

ROAST PORK SALAD

2 cups cubed, cooked pork roast
1 cup diced celery
2 Tbsp. chopped black olives
2 Tbsp. chopped pimento
Mayonnaise

Mix pork, celery, olives, and pimento. Moisten with mayonnaise. Spoon into 2 lettuce lined containers with secure lids. Keeps up to 3 days. (serves 1)

CURRIED TURKEY SALAD

2 cups cubed, cooked turkey
1 cup thinly sliced celery
½ cup finely chopped celery tops
¼ cup chopped filberts
½ tsp. curry powder
1 tsp. instant chicken bouillon
½ cup mayonnaise
1 Tbsp. lemon juice
Lettuce

Combine first 4 ingredients. Combine curry powder and bouillon with 1 Tbsp. hot water until well blended. Add to mayonnaise and beat until smooth. Add lemon juice. Pour over first mixture and toss. Chill. Spoon into lettuce lined paper bowl. Wrap securely with plastic wrap. Keeps up to 4 days. (serves 3 to 4)

TURKEY FILLING WITH HORSERADISH

1 cup diced, cooked turkey
¾ cup diced celery
⅓ cup horseradish
Dash salt and pepper
¼ cup mayonnaise

Combine ingredients and mix well. Makes enough filling for 6 sandwiches. Unused filling will keep up to 4 days.

TURKEY AND OLIVE SANDWICH FILLING

1 cup diced, cooked turkey
¾ cup diced celery
⅓ cup chopped stuffed green olives
Dash salt and pepper
¼ cup mayonnaise

Combine all ingredients and mix well. Makes 6 sandwiches. Unused filling will keep up to 4 days.

TURKEY-POCKET SANDWICHES

3 cups diced, cooked turkey
½ cup cranberry sauce
½ cup finely chopped celery
½ cup mayonnaise
¼ tsp. salt
Dash pepper
4 pita bread rounds, halved crosswise

Combine all ingredients, except bread, in mixing bowl. Spoon filling into each pita round half. Wrap each half in plastic wrap (pack 2 halves per lunch). Remaining sandwiches will keep up to 4 days.

Chapter 5

Fares Elegant

Hypothetical scene #1:
The couple, wearing T-shirts and jeans, lumbers across the grass and flops down under a tree. The girl opens a brown paper bag (okay to use under everyday circumstances, but never appropriate for a shared lunch) and extracts a couple of sandwiches carelessly wrapped in waxed paper.

"Wanna jam sandwich?" she says.

"Yeah, sure." He says.

They gobble down the sandwiches, the potato chips, and the melted chocolate bars. He rubs his chocolate-smeared mouth across the shoulder of his T-shirt while she picks at a grass stain on her levis. Later, they take turns tossing the wadded up bag at a nearby garbage can.

Suddenly she leaps up and screeches, "Last one to the cycle's a rotten egg!"

Hypothetical scene #2:
Spread beneath the shady oak is a brightly colored gingham cloth filled with the remnants of an elegant feast. An enchanted couple reach toward one another and briefly touch finger tips.

"Would you care for another glass of Chablis, mademoiselle?"

"No thank you, sir. I must guard my figure from such tempting amenities."

87   **Fares Elegant**

The gentleman packs the picnic items neatly into the wicker basket as the lady stands to smooth her frock and open her parasol. After the gentleman lifts the basket, he offers the lady his arm. They stroll across the green chatting about Elizabeth Barrett Browning's *"How Do I Love Thee"*.

When planning a lunch to be shared with another person, especially if it is plotted in the name of 'Love', setting the proper mood is nearly as important as preparing the proper food. Select the location for the affair in advance. Once the site has been picked, plan the appropriate table setting. Will a table cloth or place mats be needed? Will wine be served? Here's the chance to show off not only cooking abilities, but china dishes, silver flat ware, expensive imported cloth napkins, etc.

Remember: Don't expect the male guest to wipe his mouth with a paper napkin after relishing the Lobster Salad. The gentleman chef should provide his female guest with a rose bud or daisy to garnish her plate along with his Crab Quiche. It is tacky to serve the boss Beef Bourguignonne from a paper plate.

Most of the following recipes can be prepared the night before, so that morning finds you with plenty of time to conjure up an attractively filled basket (no bags!).

Fares Elegant

MAIN COURSES

ANTIPASTO ROLL-UPS

> 1 can (3½-oz.) tuna, drained and flaked
> 1 hard-cooked egg, chopped
> 2 Tbsp. mayonnaise
> ½ tsp. lemon juice
> 1 pkg. (6-oz.) sliced mozzarella cheese
> 1 pkg. (8-oz.) sliced party salami

Mash together tuna, egg, mayonnaise, and lemon juice; set aside. Cut each cheese slice into 4 pieces. Arrange a piece of cheese on each slice of salami, trimming cheese to fit. Spread 1 tsp. tuna mixture over the cheese. Roll up; secure with tooth-picks. (Chill. (serves 2)

ARTICHOKE-CRAB SALAD

> 4 artichoke hearts
> 4 thick slices tomato
> ½ lb. fresh crab meat
> 2 hard-cooked eggs, riced
> Lettuce
> Thousand Island dressing

Line two individual containers with lettuce. Place 2 sliced artichoke hearts on each; top with 2 tomato slices. Spoon crab meat over tomatoes and sprinkle with riced egg. Cover with tight fitting lid. Chill. Dressing should be packed in a small attractive container and spooned over salad at serving time. (serves 2)

Fares Elegant

ARTICHOKE FRITATTA

3 jars (6-oz.) each) marinated artichoke
  hearts, chopped
3 bunches green onions, chopped
1 clove garlic, minced
8 eggs, beaten
10 soda crackers, crushed
1/4 cup chopped parsley
4 cups grated cheddar cheese
Dash hot pepper sauce
Dash Worcestershire sauce
Salt and pepper to taste

Drain oil from artichokes into large skillet. Saute onions and garlic until tender. Add eggs and crackers; beat well. Stir in remaining ingredients. Pour into well oiled 11¾" x 7½" x 1¾" baking dish. Bake at 325°F. 35 minutes. Chill. Cut into squares. Keeps up to 6 days. (serves 4)

BEEF BOURGUIGNONNE

2 large onions, sliced
1/4 lb. fresh mushrooms, sliced
1 Tbsp. butter
1 lb. round steak, cut into 1½" strips
1/2 tsp. salt
1/4 tsp. crushed marjoram
1/4 tsp. crushed thyme
Dash pepper
1 Tbsp. flour
1/2 cup canned beef broth
3/4 cup red Burgundy

Saute onions and mushrooms in butter until tender; remove from skillet. Brown meat in same skillet. Sprinkle seasoning over meat. Mix flour and broth; pour into skillet and heat to boiling, stirring constantly. Stir in Burgundy. Cover and simmer 2 hours. Stir in onions and mushrooms. Pour into thermos with wide mouth. Keeps up to 4 days. (serves 4)

Fares Elegant

BOUILLABAISSE

1 Tbsp. salad oil
½ cup chopped onions
¼ cup chopped celery
1 can (16-oz.) whole tomatoes
1 clove garlic, minced
½ Tbsp. chopped parsley
½ tsp. seasoned salt
¼ tsp. thyme leaves
1½ lb. fish fillets, cut in chunks
1 dozen little-necked clams in shell
½ Tbsp. cornstarch
½ lb. shrimp, peeled and deveined

In heavy kettle, saute onions and celery in hot oil until tender. Stir in tomatoes (plus liquid), garlic, and seasonings. Cover and simmer 10 minutes. Add fish and cook 10 minutes longer.

Scrub clams. Place them in pan with ½" boiling water; cover and steam 5 minutes. Strain broth through cheesecloth, reserving 1 cup.

Blend cornstarch with clam juice; stir into tomato mixture and heat to boiling. Add shrimp and simmer 5 minutes. Add clams. Ladle into a wide mouth thermos. Unused portions may be reheated and used within 3 days. (serves 6)

CHEESE AND ONION PIE

1 9" unbaked pie shell, chilled
1 oz. grated Swiss cheese
1 oz. grated Gruyere cheese
1 oz. grated Parmesan cheese
1 Tbsp. flour
1 medium onion, thinly sliced
1 egg, lightly beaten
1 cup light cream
¼ tsp. salt
⅛ tsp. pepper
¼ tsp. nutmeg

Mix cheeses with flour. Spread the onions in bottom of pie shell, top with cheese-flour mixture. Scald cream, stir in lightly beaten egg, salt, pepper and nutmeg. Pour into pie shell. Bake at 350°F. for 30 to 35 minutes. Cool. Chill. Cut into wedges. Keeps up to 5 days.

Fares Elegant

CHICKEN-ARTICHOKE SALAD

1/2 Tbsp. butter
1/4 cup croutons
1/8 tsp. garlic salt
2 cups torn romaine
1 cup cooked chicken, cut into strips
1 can (7-oz.) artichoke hearts,
  drained and halved
1 Tbsp. grated Parmesan cheese
Caesar salad dressing

Melt butter in small skillet; add croutons. Cook and stir until croutons are lightly browned. Remove from heat and sprinkle with garlic salt. Set aside.

Combine romaine, chicken, artichokes, Parmesan, and croutons. Toss. Lightly pile salad into individual containers with tight fitting lids. Chill. Dressing should be packed in a small covered container to be poured over salad at serving time.

CHILLED HAM-LEEK QUICHE

Single 9" unbaked pie shell
1 pkg. leek soup mix
1 1/2 cups milk
1/2 cup evaporated milk
1 1/2 cups shredded Swiss cheese
3 eggs, slightly beaten
1 1/2 tsp. dry mustard
1/4 tsp. coarsely ground pepper
1 can (4 1/2-oz.) deviled ham
2 Tbsp. fine dry bread crumbs

Bake crust in 450°F. oven 7 to 10 minutes or until golden brown. Let cool.

In saucepan, stir together soup mix and milk. Cook over medium heat, stirring, until mixture boils and thickens. Stir in next 5 ingredients.

Mix together ham and bread crumbs; spread mixture over bottom of pie shell. Pour egg mixture over and bake on lowest rack at 325°F. for 60 minutes. Remove from oven; cool; then refrigerate. Cut into 6 wedges. May be packed in individual pie shaped containers. Keeps up to 4 days.

Fares Elegant

COLD POACHED SALMON STEAKS WITH SOUR CREAM

½ cup diced celery
1 carrot, cut into pieces
½ cup chopped onion
1 Tbsp. butter
½ bay leaf
1 peppercorn
1 clove
2 sprigs parsley
¼ tsp. rosemary
1 tsp. salt
½ lemon, thinly sliced
2 cups water
2 salmon steaks (5 to 6 oz. each)
Sour cream

Saute celery, carrot, and onion in butter. Add seasonings, lemon, and cold water. Bring to boil and simmer 30 minutes. Strain liquid, discarding solids. Place steaks in saucepan and cover with hot liquid. Simmer over low heat 10 minutes. Remove skin from fish and chill steaks. Place cold salmon into covered container. Spoon sour cream into smaller covered container to be served over fish at meal time. (serves 2)

CRAB RICE SALAD

1½ cups cooked rice
½ tsp. curry powder
¼ cup chopped parsley
1 Tbsp. French dressing
½ cup quartered black olives
¼ cup diced celery
1 pkg. (6-oz.) frozen crab, thawed
¼ cup mayonnaise
½ large ripe pineapple, cut lengthwise

Toss together rice, curry, parsley, and French dressing; fold in olives, celery, and mayonnaise. Refrigerate. Hollow out pineapple, leaving ½" thick shell. Refrigerate shell. Add ½ cup fresh pineapple to salad mixture.

Lightly pile salad mixture into pineapple half. Place on serving plate and wrap all in plastic wrap. (serves 2)

Fares Elegant

CRAB QUICHE

1 9" pie shell
4 eggs, beaten
2 cups light cream
2 Tbsp. minced onion
1/2 tsp. salt
1/8 tsp. cayenne pepper
1 can (7 1/2 oz.) crab meat, drained
1 cup shredded mozzarella cheese
2 Tbsp. parsley

Stir cream, onion, salt, and cayenne pepper into beaten eggs. Cover and refrigerate.

Preheat oven to 425°F. Sprinkle pastry shell with crab meat and cheese. Pour over egg mixture and sprinkle with parsley. Bake at 425°F. 15 minutes, then reduce heat to 300°F. and bake 30 minutes longer. Let cool, then chill in refrigerator. Cut into wedges and pack in wedge-shaped containers with tight fitting covers. Keeps up to 5 days.

CURRIED CHICKEN MOUSSE

1 lb. chicken breasts
1 cup water
1/2 cup sliced onion
1/2 cup fresh celery leaves
1/2 tsp. salt
2 peppercorns
1/2 envelope unflavored gelatin
1 egg, separated
1/2 cup slivered toasted almonds
1/2 tsp. curry powder
Dash pepper
1/2 cup mayonnaise
1/2 cup whipping cream
1 cup crushed pineapple
1/2 cup flaked coconut

Combine breasts, water, onion, celery leaves, salt and pepper in saucepan; simmer, covered 45 to 50 minutes. Cool. Skim, bone, and dice chicken. Strain stock, measuring out 1 cup. Soften gelatin in stock; heat, stirring, until dissolved.

Fares Elegant 94

Beat egg yolk slightly before stirring constantly for 1 minute or until slightly thickened. Remove from heat.

Stir in chicken, almonds, curry powder, and pepper; blend well. Chill 30 minutes, then blend in mayonnaise.

Beat egg white stiff; fold in chicken mixture. Pour into 4 individual gelatin molds and chill overnight.

Combine pineapple and coconut. Unmold desired serving of gelatin into lettuce lined bowls and top with pineapple and coconut.

Unused gelatin will keep up to 5 days. (serves 4)

HAM WITH ONIONS IN RAISIN SAUCE

2 thick slices lean ham
¾ lb. small white onions, peeled
2 Tbsp. olive oil
¾ cup water
¼ cup wine vinegar
½ tsp. salt
¼ tsp. freshly ground pepper
1 Tbsp. sugar
1½ Tbsp. tomato paste
¼ tsp. marjoram
1 bay leaf
½ cup raisins

Heat oil in skillet; add onions, tossing to coat. Mix in water, vinegar, salt, pepper, sugar, tomato paste, herbs, and raisins. Cover and bring to boil; cook over low heat 30 minutes. Chill. Serve over cold ham slices. (serves 2)

Fares Elegant

HAM PUFFS

2 eggs
¼ cup milk
½ tsp. dry mustard
Dash pepper
2 oz. cubed cheddar cheese
1 pkg. (3-oz.) cream cheese, cubed
½ cup finely diced ham
½ tsp. dried parsley flakes

Preheat oven to 375°F.

In blender container mix eggs, milk, mustard, and pepper. Cover; blend until smooth. Add cheese and blend until nearly smooth. Stir in ham and parsley. Pour into 4 ungreased 1 cup souffle or custard dishes. Bake 30 minutes. Cool. Wrap in plastic wrap. Serve at room temperature. Keeps up to 3 days. (serves 4)

HONEYDEW AND HAM SALAD

½ honeydew melon
½ cup cubed cooked ham
½ cup orange, peeled and sectioned
¼ cup seedless grapes, halved
¼ cup fresh, dark sweet cherries,
  halved and pitted
½ nectarine, chopped
2 Tbsp. chopped celery
¼ cup yogurt
2 Tbsp. Russian dressing

Chill ingredients thoroughly. Cut melon in half. Separate melon from shell; cut melon into pieces, returning pieces to shell. Combine ham, orange sections, grapes, cherries, nectarine, and celery. Toss to mix. Place melon halves on square of plastic wrap. Spoon ham-fruit mixture into shells and wrap plastic film over. Blend yogurt and Russian dressing. Spoon into small container to serve over Honeydew and Ham Salad. (serves 2)

Fares Elegant **96**

JAMBALAYA

2 cups cubed cooked ham
1 cup long grain rice
1 can (16-oz.) stewed tomatoes
1 pkg. (12-oz.) frozen, cleaned raw shrimp
3 Tbsp. diced onion
2 Tbsp. instant chicken bouillon
$\frac{1}{2}$ tsp. salt
$\frac{1}{4}$ tsp. thyme
$\frac{1}{4}$ tsp. chili powder
$\frac{1}{8}$ tsp. cayenne pepper
$\frac{1}{2}$ cup chopped green pepper

Cook rice according to package instructions. Add remaining ingredients and simmer 15 minutes. Spoon into wide mouthed thermos. Refrigerate unused portions. May be reheated and used within 4 days. (serves 4)

LOBSTER SALAD

$2\frac{1}{2}$ lb. frozen rock lobster tails
$1\frac{1}{2}$ qts. boiling water
$\frac{1}{2}$ tsp. salt
1 cup diced cooked potatoes
1 can (9$\frac{1}{2}$-oz.) artichoke hearts, drained
$\frac{1}{2}$ cup quartered ripe olives
$\frac{1}{2}$ cup white wine
3 Tbsp. salad oil
Dash pepper
$\frac{1}{2}$ cup mayonnaise
1 Tbsp. catsup
1 tsp. prepared mustard
$\frac{1}{2}$ tsp. salt
$\frac{1}{2}$ envelope unflavored gelatin
Few drops red food coloring
$\frac{1}{2}$ cup whipped cream
$1\frac{1}{2}$ Tbsp. horseradish
Lettuce

Place lobster in boiling water to which $\frac{1}{2}$ tsp. salt has been added; cover and simmer 10 minutes. Drain. Rinse lobster in cold water;

Fares Elegant

drain well. Remove shells from lobster and cut meat into chunks; add potatoes, quartered artichoke hearts, and olives.

In small bowl combine wine, oil, and pepper, and pour over lobster mixture; mix well. Refrigerate 1 hour.

Combine mayonnaise, catsup, mustard, and salt. Sprinkle gelatin over ¼ cup cold water, then dissolve over hot water; stir into mayonnaise mixture. Add food coloring.

Line 4 cup mold with foil, letting it extend 1" above edge. Pack in lobster mixture. Refrigerate at least 4 hours.

Whip cream stiff; fold in horseradish. Lift salad by foil edge, peel foil back about 1", then invert salad onto plate lined with lettuce leaves. Cover firmly with plastic wrap and keep cool. Serve with cream-horseradish dressing. (serves 2)

MOUSSAKA

1 - 1½ to 2 lb. eggplant, cut in 1" slices
2 Tbsp. melted butter
1 lb. ground lamb
2 Tbsp. minced onion
1 can (8-oz.) tomato sauce
½ cup red Burgundy
1 Tbsp. parsley flakes
1 tsp. salt
¼ tsp. pepper
¼ tsp. nutmeg
3 Tbsp. butter
3 Tbsp. flour
½ tsp. salt
2 eggs
1¾ cups milk
¼ cup grated Parmesan cheese
1 egg, beaten
¾ cup grated Parmesan cheese
½ cup dry bread crumbs

Cook eggplant slices in boiling water 8 minutes. Drain. Brown meat and onion in butter. Stir in 1 can tomato sauce, wine, parsley, 1 tsp. salt, pepper, and nutmeg. Cook, uncovered, over medium heat 20 minutes.

Meanwhile prepare white sauce: Melt 3 Tbsp. butter in saucepan.

Blend in flour and salt. Cook over low heat, stirring, until mixture is smooth and bubbly. Remove from heat. Blend 2 eggs into milk; stir into flour mixture. Heat to boiling, stirring constantly. Boil and stir 1 minute. Add ¼ cup Parmesan cheese. Blend well.

Stir in 1 egg, ½ cup Parmesan cheese, and ¼ cup crumbs into meat mixture. Grease 9 x 9 x 2" baking dish; sprinkle remaining crumbs evenly in dish.

Arrange ½ eggplant slices in dish; cover with meat mixture. Sprinkle 2 Tbsp. Parmesan cheese over meat and top with remaining eggplant. Pour white sauce over mixture and sprinkle with remaining cheese. Bake, uncovered, in preheated 375°F. oven for 45 minutes. Cool. Chill. Cut into squares. Serve with tomato sauce. Keeps up to 4 days. (serves 6)

PICKLED SHRIMP FILLED AVOCADO

¼ lb. frozen pre-cooked shrimp, deveined
3 Tbsp. minced sweet pickle
½ medium onion, sliced and sectioned
½ cup French dressing
1 Tbsp. pickling spice
1 large avocado

Toss together shrimp, pickles, and onion. Pour dressing over all. Tie pickling spices in cheesecloth bag and drop into center of mixture. Marinate overnight. Drain. Halve avocado and remove seed. Pile shrimp into center; place on colorful plates or bowls and wrap in plastic wrap. (serves 2)

SHRIMP STEAMED IN BEER

1 lb. uncooked shrimp, cleaned and deveined
1 can (12-oz.) beer
Cocktail sauce (recipe follows)

Place uncooked shrimp in steamer basket, pour in contents of can of beer. Cover and let beer simmer until shrimp are pink and curly. Do not over-cook. Chill. Pack in covered container. Serve cocktail sauce in separate smaller container. (serves 2 to 3)

Fares Elegant

COCKTAIL SAUCE

½ cup catsup
1 Tbsp. prepared horseradish
½ Tbsp. freshly squeezed lemon juice
Combine ingredients and chill.

SHRIMP QUICHE

3 cans shrimp
¼ lb. Swiss cheese, grated
1 pkg. (6-oz.) grated Gruyere cheese
1 Tbsp. flour
3 eggs
1 cup light cream
¼ tsp. salt
Dash pepper
¼ tsp. dry mustard
½ tsp. Worchestershire sauce
Dash hot pepper sauce
9" unbaked pastry shell

Cut shrimp in small pieces. Toss together cheese and flour. Beat eggs, cream, salt, pepper, mustard, Worchestershire sauce, and hot pepper sauce. Spread ¾ of cheese mixture in pastry shell. Add shrimp and cover with remaining cheese; pour egg mixture over cheese and shrimp. Bake at 400°F. 15 minutes; reduce heat to 325 and bake 40 minutes. Keeps up to 5 days. (serves 6)

STUFFED CORNISH HENS

½ cup minced onion
1 stalk celery, diced
2 Tbsp. butter
1 medium orange
¼ tsp. poultry seasoning
¼ tsp. salt
Dash pepper
1 cup fine dry bread crumbs
2 1-lb. Cornish game hens

Saute onion and celery in butter. Peel orange, reserving ½" square piece of peel. Quarter oranges, removing seeds. Place in blender container along with peel and seasonings. Blend until orange is coarsely chopped.

Toss celery, onion, and orange mixture with crumbs. Lightly stuff birds. Place hens, breast-side up, on rack in shallow pan. Brush with butter. Roast, covered, at 400°F. 30 minutes; uncover and roast 1 hour longer, basting occasionally with melted butter. Cool. Wrap in foil and chill. (serves 2)

Fares Elegant

STUFFED EGGS ROYAL

4 eggs, hard cooked
1 tsp. lemon juice
½ tsp. finely chopped onion
Dash salt
¼ tsp. pepper
1 cup crab meat
½ Tbsp. cream
½ cup chicken broth
2 Tbsp. butter
2 Tbsp. flour
½ cup cream
1 egg yolk, slightly beaten
¼ cup grated Parmesan cheese
2 English muffins, split
Butter

Halve eggs and carefully scoop yolks into a bowl. Add lemon juice, onion, salt, pepper, crab, and ½ Tbsp. cream to yolks. Mix to blend well. Spoon yolk mixture into egg white halves, rounding tops. Set aside.

Melt 2 Tbsp. butter in skillet, blend in flour. Heat until mixture bubbles. Remove from heat and gradually stir in broth and ½ cup cream. Return to heat and bring to a boil, stirring constantly; cook 1 to 2 minutes longer. Remove from heat and vigorously stir 3 Tbsp. of hot mixture into egg yolk, then immediately stir into sauce. Add cheese, stirring well. Place stuffed eggs into a wide-mouthed thermos; pour over sauce. Butter muffins and wrap in colorful bowls. At serving time, spoon eggs and sauce over muffins. (serves 2)

CAVIAR STUFFED ARTICHOKES

2 small artichokes
1 oz. red caviar
½ cup dairy sour cream
Lemon twists

Cut 1" from top of artichokes; trim leaves from around bottom. Slice off stem close to base. Snip off sharp leaf tips with pinking shears. Cook in boiling salted water until tender (30 to 35 minutes). Place, upside down, on rack and drain. Cool. Remove middle leaves and choke. Combine caviar and sour cream; spoon mixture into artichokes. Lightly wrap each in plastic wrap. Garnish with lemon twist at serving time. (serves 2)

TOMATOES STUFFED WITH ARTICHOKES

2 medium tomatoes
Salt and pepper
Dill weed
4 artichoke hearts, diced
2½ Tbsp. sour cream
¼ tsp. lemon juice
Dash curry powder

Cut off tops of tomatoes and scoop out seeds and juice. Sprinkle with salt, pepper, and dill. Stuff with artichoke hearts. Chill. Blend remaining ingredients. Place tomatoes in serving containers. Pack dressing in smaller container to serve over tomatoes at serving time.

Fares Elegant

DESSERTS

CHOCOLATE CHEESECAKE

1½ cups graham cracker crumbs
¼ cup brown sugar
⅛ tsp. nutmeg
⅓ cup melted butter
1 square unsweetened chocolate, melted
1 pkg. (6-oz.) chocolate chips
1 pkg. (8-oz.) cream cheese, softened
¾ cup brown sugar
Dash salt
1 tsp. vanilla
2 eggs, separated
1 cup heavy cream, whipped

Mix together cracker crumbs, ¼ cup brown sugar, nutmeg, butter, and chocolate. Press into 9" pie pan. Chill.

Melt chocholate chips over hot water. Cool 10 minutes. Blend cream cheese, ½ cup brown sugar, salt and vanilla. Beat in egg yolks, one at a time. Beat in cooled chocolate. Blend well. Beat egg whites until stiff. Gradually beat in ¼ cup brown sugar until whites are stiff and glossy. Fold chocolate mixture into beaten egg whites. Fold in whipped cream. Pour into chilled crust. Refrigerate and chill overnight. Cut into wedges. Pack in wedge shaped containers or on a serving plate. Cover lightly with plastic wrap. Keeps up to 5 days.

Fares Elegant

LEMON-CHEESE PUDDING

¼ cup sugar
1 tsp. unflavored gelatin
Dash salt
⅔ cup cold water
2 pkg. (3-oz. each) cream cheese, softened
½ cup grated lemon peel
½ cup lemon yogurt
1 Tbsp. freshly squeezed lemon juice
½ cup frozen whipped dessert topping, thawed
2 tsp. finely crushed graham crackers

Combine sugar, gelatin, and salt in saucepan. Add water. Stir over low heat until gelatin dissolves. Remove from heat. Add cream cheese, lemon peel, yogurt and lemon juice; beat until smooth. Fold in whipped topping. Pour into 4 ½-cup dishes. Sprinkle with crumbs. Cover with plastic wrap and chill until firm. Keeps up to 4 days.

MARMALADE FRUIT COMBO

3 cups honeydew melon balls
1 cup pineapple chunks
1 cup strawberries, hulled
1 can (6-oz.) grapefruit juice
⅓ cup orange liqueur
⅓ cup orange marmalade

Combine melon, pineapple, and strawberries. Chill.

Combine remaining ingredients and pour over fruit. Chill several hours, stirring constantly. Keeps 2 days. (serves 2 to 3)

PECAN TARTS

Pastry enough for 1 9" pie shell
1 egg
¼ cup sugar
2 Tbsp. melted butter
⅓ cup dark corn syrup
⅓ cup pecan pieces

Divide pastry into 6 equal portions. Form each into a ball and roll into 4" circle. Ease into muffin cup. pleating pastry for close fit.

Beat together egg, sugar, butter, and syrup. Stir in nuts. Pour into pastry. Bake in preheated 375°F. oven for 30 to 40 minutes. Cool. Wrap each in plastic wrap.

SHERRY CHIFFON PIE

Baked pastry shell for 1 9" pie
¼ cup toasted almonds. chopped
¼ cup cold water
1 Tbsp. unflavored gelatin
3 eggs, separated
1½ cups milk
⅓ cup sugar
½ cup whipping cream
¼ cup sugar
3 Tbsp. sherry
½ tsp. almond extract

Sprinkle gelatin over cold water and let stand 5 minutes to soften. Beat egg yolks slightly and set aside.

Combine milk, ⅓ cup sugar, and salt and heat in top of double boiler until milk is scalded.

Vigorously stir 3 Tbsp. of hot mixture into egg yolks. Immediately blend into mixture in top of double boiler. Cook over simmering water, stirring, until mixture coats spoon. Remove from heat.

Blend in softened gelatin. Cool; chill until mixture begins to gel.

Beat whipping cream until of medium consistency. Chill. Beat egg whites, gradually adding ¼ cup sugar, until peaks form.

Fold whipped cream and egg whites into custard mixture, along with sherry and extract. Fold in almonds. Turn into cooled pre-cooked pie shell. Chill in refrigerator 3 to 4 hours.

Cut into wedges and pack in chilled wedge-shaped containers with tight fitting lids.

107 Fares Elegant

Chapter 6

Summer Coolers

Appetites tend to lag during hot weather, so it is especially important to provide appealing lunches during hot summer months. You will find that even during the most sweltering days a Chilled Mexican Salad or generous portion of Deviled Ham Quiche is hard to pass up.

One drawback of summer lunches is that they tend to warm as the morning progresses. Packing the lunch the evening before, then refrigerating overnight is one way to chill the lunch so that it will remain cold until consumed. This doesn't apply if lunch is left in the back seat of the car with windows rolled up. However, a few lunch hours spent huddled in a small patch of shade sipping lime-flavored gelatin garnished with bits of floating pear will likely break the habit.

Chemical-filled packets are sold commercially which may be frozen and tucked in among the lunch items. Such devices are extremely effective and helpful when the noon meal is to be kept and consumed out-of-doors during hot weather.

Summer Coolers

CHILLED SOUPS

CHILLED CHICKEN SOUP

3 green outer lettuce leaves
1 can condensed cream of chicken soup
1/2 soup can water
Seasoned pepper to taste

Place all ingredients in blender container and whirl until smooth; chill. Pour into chilled thermos. (serves 1)

CHILLED CREAM OF AVOCADO SOUP

1 cup mashed ripe avocado
1 cup light cream
1 cup chicken broth
1/2 Tbsp. lemon juice
1/4 tsp. salt
Dash pepper

Combine avocado, cream, broth, lemon juice, salt, and pepper. Stir until smooth. Chill 5 hours or longer. Pour into chilled thermos.

CHILLED CREAM OF TOMATO SOUP

2 cups tomato juice
1 cup milk
1 1/2 tsp. sugar
1/2 tsp. salt
1/2 tsp. celery salt
1/2 tsp. grated onion
1/2 tsp. Worcestershire sauce

Combine juice, milk, sugar, salts, onion, and Worcestershire sauce; chill. Pour into chilled thermos.

Summer Coolers

CUCUMBER SOUP

2 medium cucumbers, peeled, seeded,
  and thinly sliced
1 cup water
1 small onion, sliced
1/2 tsp. salt
Dash pepper
1/4 cup flour
2 cups chicken broth
2 cloves
3/4 cup plain yogurt
1 Tbsp. finely chopped dill

Mix first 5 ingredients in kettle. Bring to a boil and simmer, covered, until cucumbers are soft. Puree in blender container. Make paste of flour and 1/2 cup bouillon. Gradually stir into remaining bouillon; heat. Add puree and cloves; simmer 5 minutes, stirring. Cool, then chill. Pour into thermos. (serves 2)

GAZPACHO

1 1/2 cups tomato juice
1 Tbsp. olive oil
1 Tbsp. wine vinegar
1 garlic clove
1 medium tomato, peeled and quartered
1 small cucumber, peeled and sliced
1 small green pepper, seeded and chopped
1 stalk celery, sliced
1/4 cup diced onion
2 sprigs parsley
1 slice bread, crumbled
1/2 tsp. salt
1/4 tsp. pepper

Put 3/4 cup tomato juice, oil, vinegar, and garlic in blender container. Blend until garlic is finely chopped. Add remaining ingredients and blend until vegetables are pureed (if blender container is too small, blend half at a time). Pour 1/2 into wide-mouthed thermos and chill. Remaining half will keep refrigerated up to 5 days.

Summer Coolers   **112**

SALADS

AVOCADO SALAD

1½ ripe avocados
2 slices crisply cooked bacon
½ Tbsp. pineapple juice
½ Tbsp. vinegar
½ medium tomato, diced
Lettuce leaves

Peel and mash avocados. Mix with remaining ingredients, except lettuce. Chill. Line pint-sized plastic container with lettuce. Spoon in avocado mixture and fit container with snug lid. Accompany any salad with a small package of tortilla chips. (serves 2)

CHEESE LUNCHEON PLATTER

2 slices buttered rye bread, halved
2 thick cheese slices
2 green pepper rings
1 small apple, cut in thin wedges
4 radishes
4 thick cucumber slices
1 hard-cooked egg, quartered
½ cup pecan halves
Watercress
Russian Dressing

Arrange a bed of watercress on small paper plates (2). Attractively arrange bread, cheese, and remaining ingredients, except dressing, on watercress beds. Seal plate tightly with plastic wrap. Chill. Dressing is packed in small containers to be added at serving time. (serves 2)

Summer Coolers

CHICKEN-AVOCADO TOSS

1 cup corn chips
1 small can (7½ oz.) chili with beans, heated
3 cups shredded iceburg lettuce
½ can (7-oz.) green chili sauce
½ cup shredded Parmesan cheese
6 thin slices cooked chicken
1 avocado, peeled and sliced lengthwise
4 cherry tomatoes, halved
8 black olives

Spoon chili into 2 small thermoses. Divide chips between 2 paper bowls. Toss chili sauce with lettuce and place in sandwich bags. Seal.

Combine cheese with chicken, avocado, tomatoes, and olives. Place in 2 sandwich bags and seal. To serve, place lettuce over chips in paper bowl, then add cheese-chicken mixture. Spoon over chili. (serves 2)

CHICKEN-CANTALOUPE SALAD

¼ cup bottled Italian dressing
2 Tbsp. mayonnaise
⅛ tsp. seasoned pepper
¼ cup diced celery
1 Tbsp. sliced green onion
2 cups diced cooked chicken
1 cantaloupe

Stir together dressing, mayonnaise, pepper, celery, and green onions. Add chicken; toss well. Cover and refrigerate.

Halve cantaloupe and remove seeds. Fill each half with salad. Wrap in plastic wrap and chill. When packing this salad, don't forget to include a sturdy plastic fork or spoon. (serves 2)

Summer Coolers **114**

CHILLED MEXICAN SALAD

1 lb. hamburger
1 can kidney beans, drained
1 head lettuce, shredded
2/3 cup chopped onion
4 tomatoes, sliced
2 cups corn chips
French dressing
Taco sauce

Brown hamburger in skillet; drain. Cool. Toss with beans, lettuce, onion, tomatoes, and chips. Combine French dressing with taco sauce to taste. Pack salad into 4 plastic containers with tight fitting lids. Dressing should be packed in small individual containers. Keeps up to 4 days. (serves 2)

CRANBERRY-TURKEY SALAD

1 quart cranberries
3 1/2 cups boiling water
2 cups sugar
2 Tbsp. gelatin
1/2 cup cold water
1 cup diced cooked turkey
1 cup chopped walnuts
1 cup seedless green grapes

Cook berries in boiling water, put through strainer and add sugar. Dissolve gelatin in cold water and add to the first mixture. Let stand until cool, then add remaining ingredients. Pour into 8" square pan. Chill until set, then cut into 6 portions.

To pack, place 1 portion into lettuce lined paper bowl or plastic container; cover securely. A dab of mayonnaise may be packed separately in a small container to be spooned over salad just before eating. Keeps up to 7 days. (serves 6)

CURRIED CRAB SALAD

2 cups cooked rice
¼ tsp. salt
¾ cup mayonnaise
1½ tsp. lemon juice
¾ tsp. curry powder
1 Tbsp. grated onion
1 cup crab meat
1 cup chopped celery
Tomato wedges

Combine mayonnaise, lemon juice, curry, and onion; mix well. Combine shrimp and celery in bowl, stir in mayonnaise mixture. Add rice and lightly mix with fork. Chill. Line plastic pint-sized container with lettuce. Spoon in salad and garnish with tomato wedges. May be made a day ahead of time. Unused portions will keep up to 4 days. (serves 2 to 3)

HAM-PINEAPPLE SALAD

¾ cup cubed, cooked ham
¼ cup cubed Swiss cheese
2 cups torn lettuce
½ cup seedless grapes, halved
½ cup crushed pineapple
2 Tbsp. pineapple juice
½ cup cottage cheese
1 Tbsp. lemon juice

Toss together ham, cheese, lettuce, and grapes. Pack into 2 individual containers with tight fitting lids. Chill. Put pineapple juice, cottage cheese, and lemon juice in blender container; blend until smooth. Spoon dressing into 2 small covered containers and chill. Pour dressing over salad at serving time. Keeps up to 3 days. (serves 2)

Summer Coolers

HAM SALAD BOWL

4 cups torn lettuce
1 tomato, cut in wedges
1/2 small onion, sliced and separated into rings
1/2 cup cooked cubed ham
2 hard-cooked eggs, cut in wedges
1/2 cup shredded cheddar cheese
Seasoned salt
Freshly ground pepper
2 Tbsp. Italian dressing
2 Tbsp. French dressing

Combine lettuce, tomato, onion, ham, eggs, and cheese; toss. Season to taste with salt and pepper. Mound into 2 individual containers with tight fitting lids. Combine dressings. Divide into 2 small covered containers and pour over salads at serving time. Keeps up to 3 days. (serves 2)

HE-MAN SHRIMP SALAD

1/4 cup sour cream
1/4 cup chili sauce
2 tsp. prepared horseradish
1/4 tsp. salt
1 lb. cooked, cleaned shrimp, cut-up
1 cup minced celery
Lettuce

Blend together sour cream, chili sauce, and horseradish. Stir in salt, shrimp, and celery. Spoon into 3 lettuce lined containers with tight fitting covers. Chill. Keeps up to 3 days. (serves 3)

Summer Coolers

LAMB AND MACARONI SALAD

1 cup cooked diced lamb
1½ cups cooked shell macaroni
¼ cup chopped sweet pickle
½ cup diced celery
¼ cup chopped onion
½ cup grated Cheddar cheese
½ cup mayonnaise
2 tsp. red wine vinegar
1 tsp. prepared mustard
½ tsp. salt
¼ tsp. pepper
½ tsp. celery seed

Combine lamb, macaroni, pickle, celery, onion, and cheese. Combine remaining ingredients; pour over lamb mixture and toss well. Spoon into 3 lettuce lined containers with tight fitting lids. Chill. Keeps up to 5 days. (serves 3)

MOLDED TUNA SALAD

1 pkg. (3-oz.) lemon flavored gelatin
1 cup boiling water
¾ cup cold water
1 cup drained tuna
2 hard-cooked eggs, sliced
¼ cup chopped sweet pickle
½ cup diced celery

Combine gelatin with boiling water, stir until dissolved. Add cold water. Chill until gelatin begins to set, then add remaining ingredients. Chill until set. Cut into squares. Keeps up to 7 days.

ORIENTAL SHRIMP SALAD

1 cup fresh bean sprouts
1 cup cooked cleaned shrimp
½ cup chow mein noodles
1 can water chestnuts, drained and minced
2 Tbsp. minced green onions
2 Tbsp. minced celery
¼ cup mayonnaise
2 tsp. lemon juice
2 tsp. soy sauce
½ tsp. ground ginger
Lettuce

Combine sprouts, shrimp, noodles, chestnuts, green onions, and celery. Chill.

Mix together mayonnaise, lemon juice, soy sauce, and ginger. Toss with chilled salad. Line 2 containers with lettuce and spoon in shrimp-vegetable mixture, cover tightly and chill. Keeps up to 3 days. (serves 2)

PEPPERONI-CHEDDAR SALAD

2 cups thin spaghetti, broken up
Boiling salted water
3 Tbsp. mayonnaise
1 Tbsp. prepared mustard
2 tsp. dried parsley flakes
1 Tbsp. wine vinegar
1 cup chopped tomatoes
1 pkg. (3-oz.) sliced pepperoni, quartered
½ cup cubed cheddar cheese
¼ cup diced onion
½ cup chopped green pepper

Cook spaghetti in water. Rinse in cold water and drain. Combine mayonnaise, mustard, parsley, vinegar. Add spaghetti and remaining ingredients. Toss to coat. Spoon into 3 individual lettuce lined containers, cover, and chill. Keeps up to 4 days. (serves 3)

Summer Coolers

SALMON-POTATO SALAD

  1/2 cup sour cream
  1/4 cup chili sauce
  1 Tbsp. French salad dressing
  1 tsp. lemon juice
  1 cup peeled and diced cooked potato
  1/2 cup celery
  1/4 cup diced sweet pickle
  2 Tbsp. sliced green onion
  1 cup cooked boned salmon

Combine sour cream, chili sauce, French dressing, and lemon juice. Stir in potatoes, celery, pickles, and onion. Add salmon; toss. Line 2 individual containers with lettuce. Spoon in salad, fit containers with lid, and chill. Keeps up to 3 days. (serves 2)

SHRIMP SALAD WITH AVOCADO DRESSING

  1 small ripe avocado, peeled, pitted, and diced
  1/4 cup sour cream
  1/2 pkg. (3-oz.) cream cheese
  1 tsp. lemon juice
  1/2 tsp. salt
  1 garlic clove
  Dash hot pepper sauce
  3 cups torn lettuce
  1/2 lb. cooked, shelled shrimp
  9 cherry tomatoes, halved
  2 oz. Swiss cheese, cut into strips

In blender container blend together first 7 ingredients. Divide into 3 small containers, cover, and chill. Arrange lettuce in 3 individual containers. Divide shrimp, tomatoes, and cheese among containers. Cover and chill. Pack 1 salad and 1 container of dressing per lunch. Keeps up to 3 days (serves 3)

Summer Coolers   120

SHRIMP-TOMATO ASPIC

1 pkg. lemon flavored gelatin
1 cup hot V-8 juice
1 cup cold V-8 juice
½ cup chopped green onions
½ cup chopped green pepper
1 cup drained canned shrimp

Combine gelatin with hot juice, stir until dissolved; add cold juice. Chill until partially set, then add onions, green pepper, and shrimp. Chill. Cut into squares. Place a couple of squares onto lettuce lined paper or plastic bowl. Cover with plastic wrap. Keeps up to 7 days. (serves 4 to 5)

TUNA-ARTICHOKE SALAD

1 can (16-oz.) whole green beans, drained
1 can (15-oz.) tuna, drained and flaked
½ cup sliced ripe olives
2 Tbsp. chopped pimiento
2 Tbsp. chopped anchovy fillets
¼ cup Italian dressing
2 tomatoes, sliced

Chopped beans, artichokes, tuna, olives, pimiento, and anchovy fillets. Add dressing and toss. Layer tomato slices in paper bowl and heap salad on top. Cover with plastic wrap and chill. Keeps up to 3 days. (serves 2)

TUNA-SPROUT SALAD

1 can (9½-oz.) tuna, drained and broken into large pieces
3 cups torn fresh spinach
2 cups fresh bean sprouts
1 can (5-oz.) water chestnuts, drained and sliced
2 Tbsp. sliced green onion
½ cup Russian dressing

Combine tuna, spinach, sprouts, chestnuts, and onion. Pack into 2 to 3 containers with tight fitting lids. Serve dressing in smaller containers to be poured over salad at serving time. Keeps up to 3 days. (serves 2 to 3)

Summer Coolers

TUNA STUFFED GREEN PEPPERS

3 firm green peppers
1½ cups canned tuna, drained
2 pkg. (3-oz.) cream cheese, softened
½ cup crushed pineapple, drained
1 pimiento, chopped
1 tsp. gelatin
2 tsp. pineapple juice

Combine tuna, cream cheese, pineapple, and pimento. Soak gelatin in pineapple juice and dissolve in top of double boiler over hot water. Add to tuna mixture. Slice tops off peppers and remove seeds. Pack tuna mixture into pepper shells. Chill. Wrap each separately in plastic wrap. Include plastic fork and knife when packing. Keeps up to 5 days. (serves 3)

VEGETABLE AND MEAT STICKS WITH DIP

4 thick strips of roast beef
4 thick strips cold cooked ham
2 medium carrots, peeled and cut into sticks
2 stalks celery, cut into strips
1 green pepper, cut into strips
1 medium cucumber, peeled and cut into strips
1 cup sour cream
2 Tbsp. minced green pepper
4 tsp. dry spaghetti sauce mix

Divide meat and vegetables into 2 sandwich bags. Chill.

Blend together sour cream, minced green pepper, and shaghetti sauce mix. Divide into 2 small containers, cover, and chill. At serving time, dunk meat and vegetable sticks into dip. Keeps up to 3 days. (serves 2)

COLD MAIN DISHES

BEEF-BEAN PIE

3 Tbsp. margarine
1 1/2 cups chopped onion
1 lb. lean ground beef
1 lb. fresh green beans, cooked and drained
1 tsp. salt
1/2 tsp. freshly ground pepper
1/2 tsp. nutmeg
6 eggs, beaten
1 tsp. sugar
1 1/2 Tbsp. lemon juice

Saute onion in margarine 10 minutes. Add meat and cook until no pink remains. Mix in beans, salt, pepper, and nutmeg; cook 2 minutes. Cool 10 minutes.

Beat eggs with sugar and lemon juice. Stir into meat mixture. Turn into greased 10" pie plate. Bake 325°F. 45 minutes. Cool. Cut into 5 wedges and chill. Pack in wedge-shaped containers. Keeps up to 5 days. (serves 5)

CHICKEN FILLED TACOS

4 taco shells
2/3 cup chopped onion
1 1/4 cups diced cooked chicken
1 medium tomato, chopped
1 cup shredded lettuce
1/4 cup diced black olives
taco sauce

Place onion, chicken, tomato, lettuce, and olives in individual sandwich bags. Place taco shells in paper bowls and wrap bowl in plastic wrap. Taco sauce is packed separately in small containers. Tacos are stuffed with meat and vegetables at serving time and sprinkled with sauce. (serves 2)

123   **Summer Coolers**

CHICKEN NUGGETS

2 whole chicken breasts, skinned and
   cut into 2" squares
1/4 cup dry bread crumbs, finely crushed
2 Tbsp. grated Parmesan cheese
1 tsp. monosodium glutamate
1/4 tsp. salt
1/2 tsp. dried thyme
1/2 tsp. dried leaf basil
1/2 cup margarine, melted

Combine crumbs, monosodium glutamate, salt, and herbs. Dip chicken pieces in margarine, then in crumb mixture. Place on foil-lined baking sheets and bake at 400°F. 15 minutes. Chill until ready to serve. Will keep up to 5 days. (serves 4)

COLD ROAST BEEF

3 lb. beef rolled rump roast
1 Tbsp. cracked pepper
2 Tbsp. shortening
1/2 cup water
1 tsp. instant beef bouillon

Rub roast with pepper. Melt shortening in heavy kettle; brown meat. Drain fat; pour water over roast and add bouillon. Cover and cook in 325°F. oven 1 hour. Cool. Cover and refrigerate overnight. Cut roast into thin strips and serve between sliced homemade bread, rolls, etc. Keeps up to 6 days.

CRAB PATTIWICHES

20 saltine crackers, finely crumbled
2 cans (7½-oz.) crab
4 tsp. Worcestershire Sauce
3 Tbsp. chopped parsley
3 Tbsp. mayonnaise
Dash hot pepper sauce
1½ tsp. prepared mustard
1 egg
3 Tbsp. margarine

Drain and flake crab. Combine with crumbs, Worcestershire sauce, pepper sauce, parsley, mayonnaise, and mustard. Stir until blended. Add egg and mix well. Shape into patties and fry in margarine at 350°F. in electric frying pan or hot skillet for 3 minutes on each side. Cool. Sandwich between mayonnaised bread or sesame seed buns. Unused portions keep up to 5 days. Freezes well. (serves 4)

DEEP-FRIED MEAT PIES

Pastry for 2 crust pie
⅓ cup minced green pepper
¼ cup shredded carrot
¼ cup minced celery
¼ cup minced green onion
1 Tbsp. hot red pepper
1 Tbsp. chopped parsley
1 Tbsp. chopped raisins
¼ cup canned tomato
¾ lb. ground beef
½ tsp. salt
¼ tsp. pepper
¼ cup water
2 drops hot pepper sauce
Cooking oil

Chill pastry. Combine green pepper, carrot, celery, onion, hot pepper, parsley, raisins, and tomato. Set aside. Brown beef in skillet. Drain fat. Season with salt and pepper. Add vegetable mixture, water, and hot pepper sauce. Cover and cook over low heat 30 minutes.

Summer Coolers

Fill deep saucepan ½ full with cooking oil. Heat to 375°F.

Meanwhile, roll pastry to about ½" thickness. Cut into rounds approximately 4" in diameter. Place 2 Tbsp. filling onto each round. Moisten edges, fold pastry over, and press edges together. Press edges with fork to assure tight seal.

Deep-fry pies about 3 minutes, or until golden brown, turning occasionally. Drain on paper towels. Cook. Makes about 15 pies.

DEVILED HAM QUICHE

9" unbaked pastry shell
1 can (4½-oz.) deviled ham
3 Tbsp. fine dry bread crumbs
1 cup shredded Swiss cheese
½ cup minced onion
4 eggs
2 cups light cream
½ tsp. salt
¼ tsp. sugar
⅛ tsp. cayenne

Mix ham and crumbs and spread on bottom of shell. Sprinkle with cheese and onion. Beat eggs slightly, then beat in remaining ingredients. Pour into shell and bake 425°F. 15 minutes. Reduce heat to 300°F. and bake 35 minutes longer. Remove from oven and cool. Cut into 6 wedges and chill. Keeps up to 5 days. (serves 6)

MARINATED FISH

1 lb. boneless fish fillets
Flour seasoned with salt and pepper
1/4 cup olive oil
2 green onions, minced
1/3 tsp. rosemary
1/3 cup white wine vinegar
Greek olives

Dredge fish with flour, then fry in oil until light brown. Drain on paper towels. Pour excess oil from pan, add onions, rosemary, and vinegar. Simmer and stir 3 to 4 minutes. Arrange fish in shallow baking dish; pour vinegar mixture over fish. Cover with heavy foil and refrigerate overnight.

Pack in individual containers and garnish with olives. Keeps up to 5 days. (serves 3)

OYSTER LOAF

6 slices whole wheat bread, crumbled
1 1/2 cups chopped fresh oysters
3 eggs, beaten
1/2 cup evaporated milk
1/2 tsp. salt
Dash pepper
1 tsp. poultry seasoning
3 Tbsp. minced parsley
1/2 cup minced onion
1 green pepper, finely chopped
1 Tbsp. margarine

Combine bread crumbs and oysters; mix thoroughly. Add eggs, milk, salt, and pepper; mix well.

Melt margarine in skillet. Add onion and green pepper; saute. Add oyster mixture, celery, and parsley. Mix. Turn into greased loaf pan. Bake 375°F. 30 minutes. Turn onto platter to cool. Cut into slices and wrap each slice separately. Good with lemon wedge and a side of chili sauce. Keeps up to 6 days. (serves 6)

Summer Coolers

PARMESAN DRUMSTICKS

1 cup crushed packaged herb stuffing mix
²/₃ cup grated Parmesan cheese
¼ cup chopped parsley
2 cloves garlic, minced
8 chicken drumsticks
½ cup melted margarine

Combine stuffing, cheese, parsley, and garlic. Dip drumsticks in melted margarine and roll in crumb mixture. Place pieces, skin side up and not touching, on greased cookie sheet. Bake 375°F. 1 hour and 15 minutes. Cool. Chill. Keeps up to 4 days. (serves 4)

PICKLED SALMON

2½ lb. salmon fillets
1½ Tbsp. salt
2 cups white vinegar
2 cups water
¼ cup salad oil
2 Tbsp. whole mixed pickling spice
½ tsp. salt
1 medium onion, thinly sliced

Cut fillets into 1" chunks and place in shallow glass baking dish. Sprinkle with salt and let stand 1 hour. Rinse salmon well and pat dry. Combine remaining ingredients in saucepan. Bring to a boil, reduce heat, and simmer 25 minutes. Layer salmon and onion slices in 2½ quart glass casserole. Pour boiling liquid over, cover loosely and let cool. Cover and refrigerate 24 hours. Will keep up to 10 days. (serves 4 to 6)

POTATO-BACON CUSTARD

½ cup milk
2 eggs
4 slices cooked bacon, crumbled
¼ cup onion
1 sprig parsley
¼ tsp. salt
¼ tsp. dry mustard
2 small potatoes, peeled and sliced

Put milk, eggs, bacon, onion, parsley, salt, and mustard in blender container and blend until combined. Add potato pieces, a few at a time; blend until potatoes are chopped. Turn mixture into 4 to 6 greased custard cups. Bake 350°F. 45 minutes. Cool. Chill. Keeps up to 4 days. (serves 4 to 6)

RUSKS WITH CREAM CHEESE

¼ cup margarine
2 Tbsp. sugar
2 cups whole wheat flour
¼ tsp. baking soda
¼ tsp. cream of tartar
1 egg
Cream cheese

Beat together margarine and sugar until light and creamy. Sift together flour, baking soda, and cream of tartar; add to creamed mixture alternately with beaten egg. Roll out on floured board to ¼" to ½" thickness. With 2" cookie cutter, cut into 15 rounds. Place on baking sheet and bake for 10 minutes.

Remove from oven, slice through center, return to oven and bake (cut side up) for 10 to 15 minutes. Cool. Spread with cream cheese and top with another round. Makes 15. Freezes well.

Summer Coolers

SHRIMP IN REMOULADE SAUCE

1 1/2 lbs. fresh shrimp, cooked and shelled
1 cup mayonnaise
2 tsp. prepared mustard
2 tsp. finely chopped sweet pickle
2 tsp. chopped capers
2 tsp. minced parsley
1/2 tsp. finely crushed chervil
1/2 tsp. finely crushed tarragon
1/4 tsp. anchovy paste
1 drop hot pepper sauce

Chill shrimp. Combine remaining ingredients and blend together. Place shrimp in individual containers with tight fitting lids. Pack sauce in separate covered containers. Spoon sauce over shrimp at serving time. Keeps refrigerated up to 5 days. (serves 2)

SWISS CHEESE QUICHE

1 unbaked 8" pie shell
2 cups grated Swiss cheese
8 slices bacon, cooked crisp and crumbled
1 cup cream
1/2 cup milk
3 eggs, slightly beaten
1/2 tsp. Worcestershire sauce
1/2 tsp. salt
Dash pepper
Dash cayenne pepper

Place bacon and cheese in pie shell. Scald milk and cream. Beat together eggs, Worcestershire, and seasonings. Stir in scalded cream and milk, then pour over bacon and cheese. Bake 425°F. 10 minutes. Reduce heat to 300°F. and bake 25 minutes longer. Cool, then chill. Keeps up to 6 days. (serves 5 to 6)

Summer Coolers

TUNA CHEESE PIE

1 frozen pie shell
1 can (6½-oz.) tuna
½ lb. Monterey Jack cheese, grated
2 eggs
½ cup pimento stuffed green olives
2 green onions, chopped
¼ cup sweet pickle relish

Combine tuna, cheese, eggs, olives, onions, and relish in bowl. Mix well. Spoon into pie shell and bake in preheated oven (400°F.) for 40 minutes. Chill. Cut into wedges. Keeps up to 4 days. (serves 5 to 6)

TUNA-NOODLE SQUARES

1 pkg. (8-oz.) noodles
5 eggs, beaten
1 cup sour cream
½ lb. creamed cottage cheese
½ tsp. salt
3 Tbsp. margarine
3 Tbsp. flour
1½ cups tomato juice
1 can (7-oz.) tuna

Break noodles into small pieces. Cook according to package directions. Drain. Combine with remaining ingredients and pour into greased baking dish. Bake 375°F. 30 minutes. Cool. Cut into 6 squares and chill. Remove from pan and wrap each square separately. Keeps up to 5 days. (serves 6)

ZUCCHINI QUICHE

2 cups finely diced zucchini
Salt
1½ Tbsp. butter or margarine
1 cup diced onion
1 Tbsp. flour
4 eggs, lightly beaten
1½ cups shredded Swiss cheese
2 cups light cream
½ tsp. oregano
Pinch of basil
Pepper
Pastry for 9" pie

Sprinkle zucchini with salt and let stand 30 minutes, then blot with dry paper towel. Melt butter in skillet and saute onion until tender. Add zucchini and flour; cook 1 minute. Combine in bowl with eggs, cheese, milk, oregano, basil, and pepper to taste. Pour into unbaked pastry shell and bake at 400°F. 15 minutes. Reduce heat to 350°F. and continue baking 20 minutes longer, or until quiche is set and slightly puffy. Let cool. Cut into wedges. Keeps up to 5 days. (serves 5 to 6)

Chapter 7

Winter Warmups

The office thermostat is turned down in compliance with the President's energy conservation program. You are huddled in your wool sweater but your toes are cold and your fingers are numb. Lunch break rolls around. What do you discover in the lunch bag? A cold crisp apple, a tuna sandwich loaded with Iceberg lettuce, vanilla pudding still chilled from the refrigerator, and a huge thermos of iced tea. How could a loved one do this to you? (Then again, if you packed it, you did it to yourself!)

Not all workers are fortunate enough to be employed in a chilly office. Many work outdoors amid rain, sleet and snow. Such workers may often be found attempting to chip through the ice crystals of an egg salad sandwich with chattering teeth.

Preparing a hot lunch is not difficult, and with all the improved thermos products on the market, keeping the food hot is a simple matter, also. If food is prepared the night before, it may be quickly reheated the following morning and poured or spooned into a thermos.

Imagine lunching on Hot Meatball Sandwiches while the snow hisses and lunges at the window above the desk; or, in the field, warming hands and stomach with a thermos of hot Corned Beef Chowder. Hot foods for cold weather makes sense, so why not start up a batch of Western Chili or Minestrone Soup?

Winter Warm-ups

By the way, if the recipient of the steaming lunch plans on being outdoors in wet weather, it is thoughtful to tuck a pair of dry socks and gloves in the lunch bag.

SOUPS

BEAN SOUP WITH DUMPLINGS

1½ cups dry pinto beans
5 cups water
½ cup diced salt pork
½ cup minced onion
½ tsp. salt
½ tsp. chili powder
¼ tsp. pepper
Tamale Dumplings (recipe follows)

Soak beans in water overnight. Add pork, onion, and seasonings. Bring to boiling. Reduce heat and simmer, covered, 1 hour. Remove ½ cup bean liquid, set aside to cool. Continue cooking beans until tender (1 to 1½ hours). Mash beans slightly.

Drop Tamale Dumplings into simmering beans. Cover tightly, cook 30 minutes more. Ladle into wide-mouthed thermos.

TAMALE DUMPLINGS

¼ lb. ground beef
3 Tbsp. minced onion
1 tsp. chili powder
Dash pepper
¾ cup yellow cornmeal
½ cup flour
1 tsp. baking powder
½ tsp. salt
½ tsp. sugar
½ cup cooled bean liquid

Brown beef and onion. Drain off excess fat. Stir in chili powder and pepper. Set aside to cool.

In bowl, combine cornmeal, flour, baking powder, salt, and sugar. Add bean liquid, stirring until mixture is combined.

Divide cornmeal mixture into 8 portions. With lightly floured hands, shape each portion around 1 teaspoon of meat mixture to form a ball. Stir remaining meat into beans.

Winter Warm-ups

CHEESY TUNA CHOWDER

1 Tbsp. minced onion
2 Tbsp. margarine
1 can condensed cheddar cheese soup
1/2 cup milk
1 can (16-oz.) stewed tomatoes, diced
1 can (7-oz.) water packed tuna
1 tsp. dried parsley flakes
Pepper to taste

In saucepan, saute onion in margarine until onion is tender. Add cheese soup; gradually blend in milk. Add undrained tomatoes, tuna, parsley, and pepper. Cover and simmer 10 minutes.

Ladle desired portion into thermos. Remainder will keep refrigerated up to 4 days. (serves 2)

CHICKEN CHOWDER

1/2 cup chopped onion
1 Tbsp. margarine
1 cup cooked diced chicken
1 can condensed chicken vegetable soup
1/2 cup water
1 cup cream-style corn
1/3 cup evaporated milk
1/4 tsp. pepper
Dash sage

Saute onion in margarine in saucepan. Stir in remaining ingredients. Heat to boiling. Pour into thermos.

Winter Warm-ups   **136**

CLAM-TOMATO BISQUE

1 can tomato soup
1 can (7½-oz.) minced clams
¼ tsp. salt
⅛ tsp. pepper
3 Tbsp. lemon juice
1 can rich milk
2 Tbsp. sherry

Combine soup with can of undrained clams, salt, pepper, and lemon juice. Simmer 5 minutes. Add milk and sherry. Heat but do not boil. Pour into thermos.

CORNED BEEF CHOWDER

1 can condensed cream of potato soup
3 cups milk
1 pkg. (10-oz.) frozen Brussels sprouts,
  thawed and chopped
1 can (16-oz.) corned beef, broken in pieces
1 tsp. prepared horseradish

In saucepan, blend soup and 1⅓ cups milk. Stir in sprouts; bring to boiling, stirring occasionally. Reduce heat and simmer 10 minutes. Add remaining ingredients and heat through. Ladle desired amount into thermos. Remainder keeps up to 4 days. (serves 3)

FISH CHOWDER

2 Tbsp. margarine
1/2 cup onion
1 large raw potato, chopped
1 pint tomato juice
1 pkg. (12-oz.) unthawed frozen cod, haddock,
  or flounder, cut-up
1/2 tsp. thyme
1/2 tsp. basil
Salt and pepper to taste

Melt margarine in saucepan. Add onion and potato and cook slowly, stirring occasionally, 10 minutes. Add fish pieces, bring to boil, cover and simmer 10 minutes or until fish flakes easily. Add herbs, salt and pepper. Pour into a wide mouthed Thermos. Remainder may be frozen and reheated for later use. (serves 4)

KIELBASA SOUP

1/2 cup chopped celery
1 Tbsp. butter
1 can beef broth
2 Tbsp. minced onion
1/4 tsp. dry mustard
1/4 tsp. garlic powder
1/4 tsp. dried oregano
1/4 tsp. dried basil
1/2 lb. Kielbasa sausage, sliced
1 cup canned lima beans, drained
1/2 Tbsp. cornstarch
2 tsp. cold water
1/2 cup shredded Mozzarella cheese

Saute celery in butter. Add broth, onion, mustard, garlic, oregano, and basil. Heat to boiling; stir in sausage and beans. Reduce heat and simmer, covered, 15 minutes, stirring occasionally. Combine cornstarch and water; stir into sausage mixture. Cook and stir until slightly thickened. Spoon into a wide mouthed thermos. Pack cheese in sandwich bag to sprinkle over soup at serving time. (serves 2)

Winter Warm-ups   138

LAMB AND BARLEY SOUP

A hearty soup ideal for cool, late autumn afternoons.

½ Tbsp. margarine
¾ lb. lamb shoulder, cubed
½ cup sliced green onions
½ cup sliced celery
1 small green pepper, diced
4 cups beef broth
1 cup diced potatoes
⅔ cup whole-kernel corn
½ tsp. salt
⅛ tsp. pepper
¼ tsp. thyme
¼ cup barley

Melt margarine in kettle; add lamb, onions, celery, and green pepper. Cook over low heat until lamb is browned on all sides. Add broth. Bring to a boil, then add remaining ingredients. Cover and cook over low heat, stirring occasionally, for 45 to 55 minutes. Pour into thermos with wide mouth. Remaining portions may be cooled, then frozen for later use. (serves 4 to 5)

LAMBA-BEAN SOUP

2 lamb bones
1 Tbsp. dried navy beans
¼ cup dried baby lima beans
¼ cup dried split peas
1 Tbsp. long grain rice
1 cup chopped onion
½ cup finely chopped celery
1 Tbsp. finely chopped parsley
½ cup tomato puree
3 pints water
1 tsp. salt
½ tsp. pepper

Put all ingredients in kettle. Cover and simmer 3½ hours. Remove bones, cut off meat, discarding fat, and return to pan.

Reheat desired portion and pour into thermos. Remaining soup may be frozen and kept up to 6 months or refrigerated for up to 5 days. (serves 4)

Winter Warm-ups

LENTIL SOUP

½ lb. diced bacon
1 cup diced onion
2 diced carrots
2 stalks celery, diced
2 cups diced potatoes
8 cups beef broth
Dash nutmeg
½ tsp. black pepper
1 bay leaf
1 Tbsp. flour
1 cup lentils

Saute bacon in kettle. Add onions and brown slightly. Add flour and remaining ingredients and bring to boil. Simmer and cook 2 hours. Pour desired amount into thermos. Remainder may be frozen and kept up to 6 months or refrigerated for up to 6 days. (serves 6)

MEATBALL AND VEGETABLE SOUP

¼ lb. hamburger
¼ cup bread crumbs
1 egg
½ tsp. Italian seasoning
2 Tbsp. margarine
2 cups water
½ cup green beans
2 beef bouillon cubes
1 Tbsp. minced onion
¼ tsp. dried basil
½ bay leaf
1 cup broken spaghetti
½ cup canned mixed vegetables
½ tomato, chopped

Combine hamburger, crumbs, egg, and Italian seasoning. Form into small meatballs; brown in margarine. Add remaining ingredients and bring to a boil. Simmer, covered, 20 minutes. Spoon into thermos with a wide mouth. Unused portions will keep up to 4 days. (serves 2)

Winter Warm-ups   **140**

MINESTRONE

½ cup dried kidney beans
¼ lb. bacon, diced
1 cup shredded cabbage
½ tsp. salt
¼ cup parsley, minced
1 cup carrots, grated
½ cup celery, diced
2 cloves garlic, crushed
1 medium onion, sliced
½ cup turnips, diced
¼ tsp. pepper
2 quarts chicken flavored soup stock
1 cup tomato pulp
½ cup elbow macaroni

Soak beans overnight and drain. Combine all ingredients, except macaroni, cover and simmer 1½ hours. Add macaroni and cook another ½ hour. Spoon into a wide mouthed thermos. Remainder may be frozen for later use. (serves 6)

SOUTH SEAS SOUP

½ cup sliced celery
¼ cup chopped onion
1 Tbsp. margarine
½ tsp. ground ginger
1 can cream of chicken soup
¾ cup water
¾ cup milk
2 cups diced cooked chicken
1 cup pineapple tidbits
¼ cup shredded coconut

Saute celery and onion in margarine in kettle; add ginger. Stir in soup, water, and milk. Add chicken and pineapple. Heat, but do not boil. Stir in coconut. Ladle half into a wide mouthed thermos. Unused portion will keep up to 4 days. (serves 3 to 4)

HOT SANDWICHES

BEEF-CHICKEN SLOPPY JOES

1 lb. ground beef
½ cup chopped onion
½ green pepper, chopped
2 Tbsp. prepared mustard
⅓ cup catsup
1 can condensed chicken gumbo soup
¼ cup water
Salt and pepper
4 hamburger rolls

Brown beef in skillet; drain fat and add onion and green pepper. Saute a couple of minutes; then add next 4 ingredients. Salt and pepper to taste.

Mix well, bring to a boil, cover and simmer, stirring occasionally, 30 minutes. Spoon into wide mouthed thermos.

At serving time, spoon over rolls which have been placed in paper bowls. Unused portions may be frozen and kept up to 6 months or refrigerated up to 5 days. A small amount of liquid may need to be added when reheating. (serves 4)

CHILI LAMB BURGER

¼ lb. ground lamb
½ Tbsp. margarine
1 cup kidney beans, drained
¼ cup chili sauce
¼ cup chopped onion
1 sesame seed hamburger bun

Brown lamb in margarine; drain fat. Add beans and chili sauce. through. Spoon into thermos with wide mouth. Place onion in sandwich bag and place bun in paper bowl.

To serve, split bun and spoon lamb mixture over. Sprinkle with onion. (serves 1)

143 **Winter Warm-ups**

MEATBALL SANDWICHES

1 egg, slightly beaten
1½ Tbsp. milk
¼ cup dry bread crumbs
¼ tsp. salt
½ lb. hamburger
¼ lb. sausage (ground)
½ cup chopped onion
¼ cup green pepper, chopped
½ cup tomato sauce
1 can (6-oz.) tomato paste
¼ cup cooking Burgundy
½ tsp. sugar
1 tsp. garlic powder
½ tsp. oregano
¼ tsp. rosemary
4 French rolls, split lengthwise

Combine egg, milk, crumbs, salt, beef, and sausage. Mix well. Form into 1½" balls. Brown in skillet along with onion and green pepper. Drain fat. Stir in remaining ingredients. Cover and simmer 15 minutes, stirring occasionally. Spoon desired amount into thermos with wide mouth. Place rolls in paper bowls and wrap in plastic wrap. To serve, open rolls and fill with meatball mixture. Unused portions will keep up to 5 days or may be frozen. (serves 4)

QUICK CORNED BEEF B-B-Q

¼ cup chopped onion
2 Tbsp. chopped green pepper
2 Tbsp. melted margarine
1 can (12-oz.) corned beef, flaked
¾ cup chili sauce
Hamburger buns

Saute onion and green pepper in margarine. Add corned beef and chili sauce. Stir and heat 5 to 6 minutes. Spoon desired amount into small wide mouthed thermos. Serve over split bun in paper or plastic bowl. Keep refrigerated up to 6 days. (serves 4)

SOUTHERN B-B-Q OPEN-FACES

4 lb. beef or pork roast
1 large diced onion
1 can (6-oz.) tomato paste
¾ cup water
1 cup tomato juice
½ cup brown sugar
3 Tbsp. vinegar
2 Tbsp. Worcestershire sauce
1 tsp. salt
1 tsp. paprika
½ tsp. chili powder
½ tsp. cinnamon
¼ tsp. ground cloves

Cook and shred roast. Combine remaining ingredients and simmer 15 to 25 minutes. Add meat and simmer 15 minutes more. Spoon desired amount into thermos. Serve over roll or sesame seed bun. Remainder may be placed in freezer bags and frozen for later use. (serves 6 to 8)

TACO BURGERS

¼ lb. ground beef
½ cup canned tomatoes, chopped
¼ tsp. chili powder
¼ tsp. Worcestershire sauce
¼ tsp. garlic salt
⅛ tsp. sugar
⅛ tsp. dry mustard
2 hamburger buns, split
½ cup shredded lettuce
¼ cup shredded American cheese

Brown meat in skillet; drain fat. Add undrained tomatoes, chili, Worcestershire sauce, garlic salt, and mustard. Stir well, breaking up large pieces. Bring to a boil; reduce heat. Boil gently, uncovered, until thick, 10 to 12 minutes. Spoon into a wide mouthed thermos. Pack lettuce and cheese in sandwich bags. Place buns in two paper bowls and wrap in plastic wrap. To serve, spoon meat sauce over buns, sprinkle with lettuce and cheese. (serves 2)

Winter Warm-ups

CHICKEN CURRY

1 cup chicken broth
2 cups cubed cooked chicken
½ cup minced onion
¼ cup margarine
1 Tbsp. curry powder
3 Tbsp. flour
¼ tsp. salt
⅛ tsp. pepper
1 medium tomato, peeled and quartered
Raisin English muffin
Coconut
Chopped peanuts

Combine broth, chicken, and onion. Melt butter in skillet and add curry. Stir in flour, salt, and pepper. Add chicken mixture; cook and stir until thick and bubbly.

Ladle into a wide mouthed thermos. Serve over muffins (in paper or plastic bowl) and sprinkle with coconut and peanuts. (serves 1 to 2)

CHICKEN 'N MACARONI

½ fryer, cut into serving-sized pieces
3 slices bacon
½ cup chopped onion
½ tsp. salt
2 peppercorns
3 cups water
4 oz. elbow macaroni
1 Tbsp. parsley flakes

Cook bacon in kettle, removing before it crisps. Brown chicken in bacon drippings; pour off fat. Add onion, salt, peppercorns, and water. Cover and bring to a boil, then reduce heat and simmer 2 hours. Stir in macaroni and parsley. Cook uncovered 15 to 20 minutes. Ladle half into wide mouthed thermos. Remaining portion may be cooled and frozen for up to 5 months or refrigerated for up to 4 days. (serves 2)

Winter Warm-ups   146

CHOP SUEY

½ lb. lean beef, cut into strips
1 cup sliced onions
1 Tbsp. salad oil
½ tsp. salt
1¼ cups beef broth
1 green pepper, cut in strips
½ cup diced celery
1 Tbsp. cornstarch
1 Tbsp. soy sauce
½ Tbsp. water
½ tsp. sugar

Brown meat and onion in oil in skillet. Add stock, cover pan, and let simmer 15 minutes before adding celery and green pepper. Simmer 10 minutes longer.

Combine cornstarch, soy sauce, and water. Stir into meat mixture and cook until thickened (3 to 5 minutes). Spoon into wide mouthed thermos. Serve over chow mein noodles. (serves 2)

CREAMED CORNED BEEF ON CORN BREAD

1 can (3-oz.) mushrooms in butter sauce
Milk
1 pkg. (2-oz.) white sauce mix
¼ cup dry white wine
¼ cup grated Parmesan cheese
Dash paprika
6 oz. corned beef, chopped
¼ cup cooked peas, drained
Corn bread squares

Drain mushrooms, reserving liquid. Add enough milk to mushroom liquid to make ¾ cup. Prepare white sauce mix, using mushroom-milk liquid and wine. When sauce is thickened, stir in cheese, paprika, mushrooms, beef, and peas. Heat thoroughly.

Spoon into small wide mouthed thermos. Serve over corn bread in plastic or paper bowl. Keeps refrigerated up to 4 days. (serves 2)

CREAMED HAMBURGER OVER CORN BREAD

1 lb. hamburger
1 can cream of mushroom soup
1½ soup can milk
Corn bread squares

Brown meat. Drain excess grease and stir in soup and milk. Heat. Spoon into a wide mouthed thermos. Wrap plastic wrap around corn bread in paper bowl. Spoon creamed hamburger over corn bread at serving time. Unused portion may be kept and reheated within 4 days. (serves 4)

CURRIED EGGS

3 hard-cooked eggs
2 Tbsp. margarine
2 Tbsp. flour
¼ tsp. salt
¼ tsp. curry powder
⅛ tsp. pepper
1 cup warm milk

Make white sauce by melting margarine in skillet, then stirring in flour and seasonings. Gradually add milk. Cook over medium-low heat until sauce has thickened. Slice eggs and heat in sauce. Spoon into small wide mouthed thermos. Serve over split English muffins or raisin bread. (serves 1 to 2)

CURRIED MACARONI AND SHRIMP

2 Tbsp. margarine
1 cup chopped peeled apple
1/2 cup sliced celery
3/4 tsp. curry powder
1 chicken bouillon cube
2 cups water
1 pkg. (7 1/2-oz.) macaroni and cheese
1/4 tsp. salt
3/4 cup evaporated milk
1 can (4 1/2-oz.) shrimp, drained

Melt margarine in skillet, then add apple, celery, and curry. Cook until apple and celery are tender-crisp. Remove from heat.

Add bouillon cube, water, macaroni from mix, and salt. Return to heat. Cook, covered, until macaroni is tender. Stir in package of cheese from mix, milk, and shrimp. Heat through. Spoon into small wide mouthed thermos. Remainder will keep up to 5 days. To reheat, add a small amount of milk to desired amount and heat over medium-low heat, stirring constantly. (serves 4)

HOT DOG POTATO SALAD

1 can (10-oz.) cream of celery soup
1/4 cup milk
2 Tbsp. sweet pickle relish
2 Tbsp. vinegar
2 Tbsp. finely chopped onion
1/4 tsp. salt
3 cups diced, cooked potatoes
5 frankfurters, sliced into 1" pieces

In skillet, combine first six ingredients; cook and stir until boiling. Stir in potatoes and franks; heat through. (serves 4)

Winter Warm-ups

HOT HAM-POTATO SALAD

2 1/2 cups cubed cooked potatoes
1/2 cup chopped cooked ham
1/2 can (11-oz.) condensed cream of celery soup
1/4 cup finely chopped onion
2 Tbsp. vinegar
1 Tbsp. sweet pickle relish
1 Tbsp. chopped pimento
1/2 Tbsp. sugar
1/2 tsp. celery seed
1/4 tsp. salt

Place potatoes and ham in skillet. In bowl, combine remaining ingredients and pour over potato-ham mixture and cool over low heat 2 hours or until potatoes are tender. Spoon desired portion into a wide mouthed thermos. Remainder will keep up to 5 days. (serves 2)

IRISH STEW

1 lb. cubed boneless lamb
1/4 cup flour
1 tsp. salt
Dash pepper
2 Tbsp. cooking oil
1/2 qt. water
1 cup diced onion
2 stalks celery, sliced
2 small carrots, sliced
3 medium-sized potatoes, quartered
1 small turnip, quartered
1 tsp. concentrated meat extract
1/4 cup water
2 Tbsp. flour
Salt and pepper, to taste

Mix together 1/4 cup flour, salt, and pepper in plastic bag. Add meat and shake to coat. Heat oil in kettle; add meat and brown on all sides. Drain and add water. Cover and bring to boil over high heat. Reduce heat and simmer gently 1 hour.

Winter Warm-ups   **150**

Add vegetables and cover. Simmer 45 minutes. Dissolve meat extract in small amount of hot water, then stir into stew. Combine 1/4 cup water and 3 Tbsp. flour; mix well. Slowly stir into simmering liquid. Spoon into a wide mouthed thermos.

Unused portions may be frozen for later use or kept refrigerated for up to 5 days. (serves 4)

MACARONI 'N BEEF

3 cups elbow macaroni
Boiling water
1/2 lb. ground beef
1 can (8-oz.) tomato sauce
1 can (8-oz.) jellied cranberry sauce
1/4 cup water
1/4 cup barbecue sauce
1/4 tsp. salt
1/2 tsp. ground ginger
1/4 tsp. ground cinnamon

Cook macaroni in boiling water until tender. Drain and rinse. Brown meat in skillet; drain excess liquid. Stir in remaining ingredients. Cook, uncovered, over medium heat 12 to 15 minutes. Stir in macaroni. Spoon into thermos with wide mouth. Unused portions will keep up to 5 days. (serves 3 to 4)

ORIENTAL MEATBALLS

1/2 lb. ground beef
1/4 cup bread crumbs
1 small clove garlic, minced
1 Tbsp. soy sauce
1 egg
1 small can water chestnuts, chopped

Mix well and make walnut-sized meat balls. Roll in 2 Tbsp. cornstarch and saute in 2 Tbsp. oil. Remove meat balls and add to pan drippings 1/4 cup sugar, 1/4 cup vinegar, 1/4 cup pineapple juice and 3/4 cups pineapple chunks. Simmer meat balls in sauce 10 minutes. Spoon half into a wide mouthed thermos. Place 1 1/2 cup chow mein noodles in plastic or paper bowl; cover with plastic wrap. To serve, spoon meatballs over noodles. (serves 2)

Winter Warm-ups

SAUSAGE SCALLOP OVER CORN BREAD

½ cup chopped celery
2 Tbsp. minced onion
½ lb. bulk pork sausage
1½ Tbsp. cold water
1½ Tbsp. flour
¼ tsp. salt
¼ tsp. paprika
¾ cup milk
Corn bread

Put celery, onion, sausage, and cold water in heavy skillet. Cover and simmer 10 minutes. Drain fat, reserving 1 Tbsp. Remove sausage and vegetables from skillet and set aside.

Return reserved fat to skillet. Blend in flour, salt, and paprika. Heat until mixture bubbles. Remove from heat. Gradually add milk, stirring constantly. Return to heat and bring to a rapid boil, stirring continuously. Cook 1 to 2 minutes longer. Add sausage mixture and heat.

Spoon into a wide mouthed thermos. Serve over corn bread. (serves 2 to 3)

TOMATO RAREBIT

2 Tbsp. flour
2 Tbsp. butter
1 cup milk
1 cup thick tomato juice
Pinch of baking soda
1 cup grated sharp cheddar cheese
1 egg
Crackers

In top of double boiler blend flour, butter, and milk. Heat tomato juice with baking soda in a small pan. Add cheese to the first mixture; then add heated tomato juice. Add 1 beaten egg and season to taste with Worcestershire sauce, hot pepper sauce, paprika, etc. Pour into a wide mouthed thermos and serve over crackers. (serves 2)

WESTERN CHILI

3 slices bacon
2 lb. stew meat, trimmed
1 large onion, chopped
2 cloves garlic, minced
2½ Tbsp. chili powder
Salt and pepper to taste
1 tsp. oregano leaves
1 tsp. ground cumin
4 cups water
4 beef bouillon cubes
1 cup dried red beans
4 cups grated carrots

In 5 qt. kettle, cook bacon crisp; remove and set aside. Reserve 3 Tbsp. drippings. Saute meat in reserved drippings, a few pieces at a time. Add onion and garlic and cook until limp. Stir in seasonings, water, bouillon, and beans. Cover and simmer 2 hours. Skim fat. Heat to boiling and add carrots. Cover and simmer 30 minutes longer. Keeps up to 6 days. (serves 6)

Winter Warm

Chapter 8

Bagging It Naturally

The thought of eating natural foods makes some folks feel uncomfortable. Why? Because alfalfa sprouts ("Alfalfa gives me hay-fever."), brewer's yeast (I get all the yeast I need from Grandpa Dick's Fluffy White Bread), and lentils (Lentil? Isn't that a religious observation?) are foreign to many.

Natural food fanciers are equally leary of consuming such things as sodium aluminum phosphate or potassium hydroxide—neither of which is included in this chapter.

Natural food is not only healthful, but interesting, too. Even young children welcome Orange Buttermilk Nog and Molasses-Nut Custard. If you have failed to try natural foods as lunch box fillers, now's the perfect time to incorporate some into your family's eating habits. As for those of you who have made natural foods an important part of your life, here are some recipes you have yet to discover!

155 **Bagging It Naturally**

BEVERAGES

BANANA SOY MILK

4 heaping Tbsp. soybean powder
1 pint water
1 large banana
1 Tbsp. honey
½ tsp. vanilla
1 Tbsp. malt

Place ingredients in blender container and blend well. Chill. Pour into chilled thermos.

CARROT JUICE

3 cups carrots, peeled and sliced
1 tsp. vegetable salt
1½ Tbsp. lemon juice, freshly squeezed

Whirl carrots, 1½ cups water, and salt in blender until pureed. Strain through cheesecloth, pressing to extract all juice. Add lemon juice and chill.

FRESH TOMATO JUICE

Put cut-up ripe tomatoes in blender (if tomatoes are not juicy, add a small amount of water). Whirl until smooth, then put through strainer. Season to taste with vegetable salt and pepper.

Bagging It Naturally

GREEN DRINK

1 cup unsweetened pineapple juice
1 Tbsp. sunflower seeds
¼ cup fresh parsley
¼ cup alfalfa sprouts

Place all ingredients in blender container and puree 3 minutes. Chill. Pour into chilled thermos.

ORANGE BUTTERMILK NOG

2 cups freshly squeezed orange juice
2 cups buttermilk
¼ cup honey
3 eggs
Dash nutmeg

Combine all ingredients in blender. Whirl 1 minute. Pour into chilled thermos.

AVOCADO-SWISS SANDWICH

1 small avocado
2 slices Swiss cheese
1 cup alfalfa sprouts
1 Tbsp. mayonnaise
4 slices whole-grain bread

Peel and pit avocado; mash pulp. Spread mayonnaise on bread slices, then add avocado on two slices. Top with Swiss cheese and sprouts. Add remaining bread slices. (makes 2)

FRUIT AND CHEESE SALAD

1/2 avocado, peeled, pitted, and cut into strips
1 Tbsp. lemon juice
1 1/2 cup melon balls
1/2 cup fresh pineapple cubes
1/2 cup halved strawberries
1/2 cup cheddar cheese cubes
1/2 cup yogurt
1 Tbsp. honey
1 Tbsp. pinyon nuts

Sprinkle avocado with lemon juice. Combine with melon, pineapple, strawberries, and cheese. Toss well. Spoon into two lettuce lined containers with tight fitting lids. Chill.

Combine yogurt, honey, and nuts; mix well. Pack in small containers to be served over salad at serving time. Keeps up to 2 days. (serves 2)

Bagging It Naturally

GREEK STUFFED TOMATOES

> 2 large firm tomatoes
> 1/2 tsp. sea salt
> Dash freshly ground pepper
> 1/4 cup olive oil
> 1/4 cup chopped onions
> 2 Tbsp. raw brown rice
> 1 Tbsp. raisins
> 1/4 cup boiling water
> 1/2 Tbsp. minced parsley
> 2 Tbsp. pinyon nuts
> 3 Tbsp. dry whole-grain bread crumbs

Cut 1/2 slice off top of tomatoes; reserve tops. Scoop out as much pulp as possible. Sprinkle inside with salt and pepper; chop pulp.

Saute onion in oil. Stir in rice, pulp, raisins, and water and cook over low heat 10 minutes. Mix in parsley and nuts. Stuff tomatoes loosely, sprinkle with crumbs and replace tops. Arrange in oiled baking dish and bake 350°F. 45 minutes. Cool. Chill in refrigerator. Keeps up to 4 days.

LENTIL LOAF

> 1 cup dried lentils
> 4 cups water
> 1 1/2 cups dry whole-grain bread crumbs
> 1/4 cup tomato paste
> 3 Tbsp. milk
> 1 egg, slightly beaten
> 2 Tbsp. vegetable oil
> 1 tsp. vegetable salt
> Dash pepper
> 1 tsp. sage
> 3 Tbsp. minced parsley
> 1 cup minced onion

Soak lentils in water overnight. Simmer in soaking water until soft. Force through a sieve. Combine remaining ingredients and mix thoroughly. Turn into greased loaf pan. Bake 425°F. 25 minutes. Baste occasionally with 2 Tbsp. butter melted in 3 Tbsp. hot water. Cool. Slice loaf, wrap each slice individually and chill. May be frozen and kept up to 6 months or refrigerated for up to 6 days. (serves 4)

NAVY BEAN SOUP

1 cup navy beans
2 cups water
2 cups carrot juice
1 cup chopped onion
2 carrots, sliced
1/2 cup diced celery
1/4 cup minced green pepper
2 ripe tomatoes, pureed
1/2 tsp. vegetable salt
1 clove
2 peppercorns

Wash beans; cover with water and soak overnight. Drain. Place 2 cups water, juice, and remaining ingredients in pressure cooker. Cook 30 minutes at 15 lbs. Keeps up to 5 days.

NUT-CHEESE PATTIES

1/4 cup dry whole-grain bread crumbs
1/4 cup pecans
2 Tbsp. grated cheddar cheese
1/4 cup chopped onion
1/4 tsp. sea salt
1/2 Tbsp. dried parsley
Dash sage
2 small eggs, beaten well
1/2 Tbsp. butter
1/4 cup tomato juice

Force nuts, cheese, and onion through food chopper, using finest blade. Combine with bread crumbs and seasonings; regrind. Add eggs and mix well. Form into 3 small patties and saute in melted butter. Add juice and simmer, uncovered, 10 minutes. Spoon into small wide mouthed thermos. (serves 1)

Bagging It Naturally

PECAN-NUT LOAF

1 cup hot cooked rice
1 cup pecans, finely chopped
1 cup cracker crumbs
1 egg, well beaten
1 cup milk
1 tsp. salt
¼ tsp. pepper
1 Tbsp. melted margarine

Mix rice, nuts, and crumbs; then add egg, milk, salt, and pepper. Turn into well greased bread pan; pour over margarine, cover and bake at 350°F. 60 minutes. Turn onto platter and cool. Slice into serving-sized portions and wrap each separately.

TABULI

½ cup bulgar wheat
Boiling water
½ cup tomato, peeled and chopped
¼ cup chopped parsley
¼ cup chopped mint leaves
¼ cup onion, chopped
¼ cup olive oil
2 Tbsp. lemon juice
½ tsp. vegetable salt
Dash pepper

Place cracked wheat in oven-proof bowl and pour in boiling water to cover. Let stand 2 to 2½ hours; drain well. Add tomato, parsley, mint, and onion. Combine remaining ingredients in jar with tight fitting lid; shake well to mix. Pour over wheat mixture, toss lightly. Chill overnight to blend flavors.

Line covered container with lettuce leaves. Spoon in Tabuli and cover. (serves 1 to 2)

VITALITY SOUP

2 bunches celery
12 medium carrots
1 lb. spinach
2 onions, quartered
1 bunch parsley
2 quarts water
1 Tbsp. vegetable salt
4 cups tomato juice

Scrub carrots and celery; cut into 1" pieces. Puree' celery, carrots, spinach, onions, and parsley in blender, using part of the 2 quarts of water, if needed. Add remaining ingredients and bring to a boil over medium heat; reduce flame and simmer 10 minutes. Good hot or chilled. Keeps 1 week refrigerated or 6 months frozen. (serves 4 to 5)

Bagging It Naturally

WHOLEWHEAT-CHEDDAR BREAD

2¹/₂ cups whole wheat flour
1 tsp. baking powder
1 tsp. baking soda
¹/₂ tsp. sea salt
2 cups shredded cheddar cheese
1 cup chopped nuts
1 Tbsp. grated orange peel
1 egg, slightly beaten
1 cup milk
¹/₄ cup butter, melted
¹/₄ cup molasses
¹/₂ cup honey

Sift together flour, baking powder, soda, and salt; add cheese, nuts, and peel. Blend thoroughly. Combine egg, milk, butter, molasses, and honey; add all at once to dry ingredients and stir only until blended. Spread on greased and floured 9¹/₂ x 5¹/₄ x 2¹/₂" loaf pan. Bake 350°F. 45 minutes. Keeps up to 5 days. May be frozen.

FRESH MUSHROOM-YOGURT SOUP

> ¼ cup margarine
> 2 bunches green onions, chopped (tops included)
> ¾ lb. fresh mushrooms, sliced
> 2 tsp. paprika
> ¼ cup flour
> 6 cups chicken broth
> 2 egg yolks
> 1½ cups unflavored yogurt
> ¼ tsp. dried rosemary

Saute green onions in melted margarine over medium-high heat. Add mushrooms and cook until mushrooms are soft. Stir in paprika and flour, then gradually stir in broth; cook, stirring, until thickened. Cover and simmer for 30 minutes.

Beat egg yolks lightly with yogurt and rosemary. Stir 1 cup of hot soup into egg mixture. Return to soup and cook, stirring, over low heat until just thickened; do not allow to boil. Spoon into thermos. Keeps up to 3 days. (serves 6 to 7)

HOMINY SPOON BREAD

> ½ cup hominy grits
> 2½ cups boiling water
> 3 Tbsp. butter
> 4 eggs, well-beaten
> 1 pink milk
> 1 cup corn meal
> 2 tsp. vegetable salt

Slowly stir hominy grits into boiling water. Cook slowly. Add butter and stir in eggs. Gradually add milk; stir in corn meal and salt. Pour into greased baking dish and bake 50 minutes at 400°F.

POTATO CHIPS

Slice desired amount of unpeeled potatoes very thin, then soak slices in ice water 1 hour. Drain and pat dry with paper towels. Spread slices on cookie sheet sprinkled with vegetable salt and bake at 500°F. until lightly browned, turning once.

PRUNE BROWN BREAD

⅔ cup corn meal
1⅓ cups sifted whole wheat flour
1 tsp. baking soda
1 tsp. sea salt
⅔ cup plumped, pitted, chopped prunes
1⅓ cups buttermilk
½ cup molasses

Sift together corn meal, flour, soda, and salt. Stir in prunes. Combine buttermilk and molasses; stir into dry ingredients just enough to moisten. Pour into 2 well-greased round 1 lb. cans. Cover tightly with square of heavy foil. Place cans on rack in deep saucepan. Pour in 3" of boiling water. Cover and steam 2 hours or until firm. Cool 10 minutes before removing from cans. Chill. Slice and spread with desired filling.

RAISIN BROWN BREAD

3½ cups whole wheat flour
1½ Tbsp. baking soda
1 Tbsp. sea salt
½ cup corn meal
⅔ cup raisins
1 cup molasses
1 egg, beaten
2 cups milk
½ cup melted butter

Sift together flour, soda, salt, and corn meal. Gradually mix in raisins, molasses, egg, milk and butter. Pour into 2 greased bread pans. Bake 325°F. 55 to 60 minutes.

Bagging It Naturally

RAW VEGETABLES WITH DIP

1/2 pint yogurt
1/2 Tbsp. horseradish
1/2 Tbsp. paprika
1/2 Tbsp. minced chives
1/2 tsp. sea salt
1/2 tsp. tarragon
1/2 tsp. grated garlic

Blend ingredients thoroughly and chill well. Clean and soak in ice water raw carrot sticks, raw cauliflowerettes, radish roses, celery sticks, cucumber sticks, etc. Spoon dip into 2 containers with tight fitting lids and chill. Place dip container, along with bag of chilled vegetables in lunch bag. (serves 2)

SOYBEAN NUTS

1 cup dry soybeans
3 cups water
1 tsp. peanut oil
1/4 tsp. salt

Soak soybeans in water overnight in refrigerator. Drain well and dry with paper towels. Spread soybeans on a cookie sheet and roast in 300°F. oven for 2 hours, stirring occasionally. Place under broiler and continue to roast, stirring frequently until soybeans are browned (4 to 5 minutes). Toss with peanut oil and salt. Store in covered container.

STEAMED CORN BREAD

1 cup graham flour
1 cup corn meal
1½ cups yogurt
1½ tsp. baking soda
½ cup molasses
½ cup raisins

Mix flour and corn meal. Add remaining ingredients and mix until blended. Spoon into 3 1-lb. cans. Cover tops with aluminum foil and secure with string. Steam on rack in kettle (with water touching bottoms of cans) 1¼ hours. Cool. Remove from cans and slice.

YEAST SPREAD

1 cup tomato juice
2 Tbsp. soy sauce
¼ Tbsp. powdered celery seed
¼ tsp. powdered onion
Brewer's yeast

Bring first 4 ingredients to a rolling boil. Cool. Mix with enough yeast to make spreading consistency. Good on crackers or bread.

DESSERTS

CAROB CARAMELS

1 cup coconut
½ cup carob powder
1 cup soy milk powder
¾ cup honey
1 tsp. vanilla
2 Tbsp. butter
1 tsp. grated orange rind
Finely chopped nuts

Sprinkle bottom of flat pan with finely chopped nuts. Combine remaining ingredients and spread mixture over nuts, pressing firmly and smoothly into pan. Sprinkle nuts over top and pat down. Cut into oblong pieces and chill.

DATE-BRAN MUFFINS

2 cups whole wheat flour
3½ tsp. baking powder
1 tsp. sea salt
½ cup honey
2 cups wheat bran
1 cup chopped dates
¾ cup chopped walnuts
1 egg, beaten
1¼ cups milk
⅓ cup melted butter

Sift together flour, baking powder, and salt. Add honey, bran, dates, and nuts. Combine beaten egg, milk, and butter. Add to dry ingredients and mix quickly. Fill paper lined muffin tins ⅔ full. Bake 350°F. 35 to 40 minutes.

Bagging It Naturally

FRUIT FILLED ORANGE

1 orange
½ cup fresh pineapple tidbits
½ cup fresh strawberries, sliced
¼ cup snipped pitted dates
½ Tbsp. honey
1 tsp. lemon juice

Cut orange in half and hollow out shell. Remove excess white membranes from orange pulp. Slice fruit, reserving juice. Combine diced orange, pineapple, strawberries, and dates.

Combine honey, and lemon juice with orange juice. Pour over fruit. Fill orange shells with fruit mixture, wrap in plastic wrap and place in paper bowl. (serves 2)

INDIAN PUDDING

1 quart milk
1 cup raisins
½ cup molasses
½ tsp. sea salt
9 Tbsp. dark farina
6 Tbsp. toasted wheat germ
½ tsp. cinnamon
½ tsp. nutmeg
2 eggs

Heat 3 cups of milk in top of double boiler and bring to boil. Add raisins, molasses, and salt. Combine farina, wheat germ, and spices; mix well. Gradually stir in boiling milk, stirring constantly until thick. Remove from heat. Combine eggs with remaining milk and gradually stir into cooking cereal mixture. Turn into greased 1½ quart casserole. Bake 350°F. 30 minutes. Chill. Spoon desired portion into serving-sized container with tight fitting lid. Keeps up to 5 days.

MOLASSES-NUT CUSTARD

½ cup raisins
½ cup chopped wlanuts
6 slices whole-grain bread, cubed
3 eggs
½ cup molasses
3 cups whole milk
½ tsp. nutmeg
1 tsp. cinnamon

Break eggs into large mixing bowl and beat with electric mixer until frothy. Add molasses, milk, and spices and beat until thoroughly mixed. Arrange alternate layers of bread and raisins in greased baking dish, ending with bread layer. Pour egg mixture over. Let stand a few minutes until bread absorbs liquid. Sprinkle with nuts. Bake 325°F. 1 hour. Chill. Cut into squares. Keeps up to 6 days.

PEANUT KISSES

½ cup molasses
½ cup peanut butter
¼ cup chopped peanuts
½ cup chopped dates
1 cup soy milk powder

Combine all ingredients and knead well. Add more soy powder if needed to form a stiff dough. Roll out and cut into squares. Keep refrigerated.

Bagging It Naturally

PRUNE PUDDING

1 cup prune juice
1 Tbsp. cornstarch
3 Tbsp. honey
1 1/4 cup chopped pitted prunes
1 Tbsp. butter
2 Tbsp. lemon juice
1 cup cream

Heat juice and thicken with cornstarch. Cook 10 minutes and add honey and prunes. Cook 5 minutes. Remove from heat and add butter and lemon juice. Chill. Spoon into individual containers with tight fitting lids. Before packing for lunch, pour over 1/4 cup cream per container. (serves 4)

Chapter 9

Kid Pleasers

Have you ever tried to supervise the consumption of a child's lunch away from home? As the child rushes out the door your words echo after him: "Eat your bread crusts. Finish the sandwiches before the cookies! Don't forget to drink your millllllk!"

Then, after school, while the kid is trying to divert your attention with a green and pink turkey he colored in art, you relieve the lunch box of its still neatly wrapped sandwiches, wipe the pulverized banana from the full thermos of milk and search in vain for the cookies. An interrogation takes place as to what the child did during lunch break and it is found that a large part of it was spent watching some boy wind strands of a little girl's hair around a cucumber stick. During the course of the conversation it's also discovered that the corned beef sandwich lavished with horseradish was not the hit it had been when served to the man of the house.

The situation isn't as hopeless as it appears. With a little ingenuity you can make the opening of a home packed lunch enticing. Once the child begins to look forward to opening the lunch box, be certain the food found there grabs his interest. Here are some suggestions to make certain the lunch is opened: 1) Use a felt-tipped pen to draw a funny face on the hard-cooked egg. 2) Print a silly lyric on the napkin. 3) Hide a small trinket among the

175   **Kid Pleasers**

food. 4) Provide a novelty straw for drinking milk. Now it's your turn. Go ahead, give it a try. 5) . . . ?

Now, about the food. First of all, lunch away from home is not the time to introduce new tastes to an inexperienced palate. Unfamiliar foods are likely to be eyed with suspicion. It is not an unusual lunch room scene to see several children crowded around a lunch box, containing an unidentifiable tidbit, discussing methods dealing with its disposal. Therefore, keep food familiar.

Second, know your child's likes and dislikes. This is relatively simple since children have a limited vocabulary relating to he subject — "mmmm" and "yuck" (often followed with an "I think I'm going to throw up" added for drama).

The following recipes have drawn far more 'mms' than 'yucks' from children sampling them. Throw a few at your kids and see what happens.

Kid Pleasers   **176**

BEVERAGES

CARROT MILK

2 cups milk
3 medium carrots, peeled and grated
Put milk and carrots in blender container and blend until carrots are liquified. Chill thoroughly before pouring into thermos.

CHERRY-LIME DELIGHT

1 can (60oz.) frozen black cherry drink,
  reconstituted
1 can (6-oz.) frozen limeade, reconsistuted
Combine ingredients and chill thoroughly before pouring into thermos.

MAPLE-NUT MILK

1 qt. milk chilled
2/3 cup maple-flavored syrup
1/2 cup creamy peanut butter
1 tsp. maple flavoring
Put all ingredients into blender and blend until smooth. Pour into thermos.

RASPBERRY FILP

1 qt. milk, chilled
1 cup red raspberry preserves
Blend in blender at high speed 30 seconds. Pour into chilled thermos.

177   **Kid Pleasers**

MAIN COURSES

CHILI SPAGHETTI

1 1/2 Tbsp. cooking oil
1/2 cup chopped onion
3/4 lb. ground beef
1 3/4 cups canned tomatoes, diced
1 1/4 cups cooked, drained kidney beans
1/2 Tbsp. chili powder
3/4 tsp. salt
1/2 tsp. sugar
1/4 tsp. pepper
2 qts. water
2 tsp. salt
1 cup uncooked spaghetti (broken into 3" pieces)

Brown beef and onion in oil. Drain excess fat. Stir in tomatoes, beans, chili, salt, sugar and pepper. Cover and simmer 45 minutes.

Bring water to boil. Add salt and spaghetti and cook 10 to 15 minutes. Drain and rinse spaghetti, then add to cooked chili mixture. Heat. Spoon into a wide mouth thermos. Serves 2.

Unused portions keep up to 5 days. A small amount of water needs to be added when reheating.

CORN-CRISPED DRUMSTICKS

1 cup corn flakes, rolled into fine crumbs
1 tsp. monosodium glutamate
1/2 tsp. salt
1/4 tsp. pepper
6 chicken drumsticks
1/2 cup evaporated milk

Combine crumbs, monosodium glutamate, salt and pepper in shallow dish. Line baking pan with foil. Dip drumsticks in milk, then roll in seasoned crumbs. Place on foil and bake 350°F. 1 hour. Cool, then chill. Serves 3.

Kid Pleasers

CREAMED CHICKEN OVER ROLLS

    2 cups cooked, cubed chicken
    1 can cream of chicken soup
    ½ soup can milk
    Potato rolls

Combine chicken, soup and milk in saucepan. Heat. Spoon into a wide mouth thermos. Split tolls and place in paper bowls. Wrap with plastic wrap. Spoon creamed chicken over rolls at serving time. (serves 2)

HOT DOGS

    2 frankfurters
    2 hot dog buns
    1 Tbsp. mustard
    1½ Tbsp. catsup
    Margarine

Spread margarine on inside of buns. Combine mustard and catsup; spread over margarine. Sandwich bun halves together and wrap in plastic wrap. Put frankfurters in a wide mouth thermos then fill thermos with boiling water. At lunch, open thermos, remove hot frankfurter and place between bun. (serves 1)

MACARONI 'N CHEESE SALAD

    2 cups shell macaroni
    1 cup cubed American cheese
    1 green pepper, seeded and chopped
    4 small carrots, grated
    3 stalks of celery, cut fine
    ½ tsp. salt
    Mayonnaise

Cook macaroni 15 minutes, drain and cool. Add to cheese, green pepper, carrots, celery and salt. Mix well. Moisten with mayonnaise and pack into three individual containers with tight fitting lids. (serves 3)

Kid Pleasers   **180**

PEANUT BUTTER-BANANA SANDWICH FILLING

1 banana, mashed
1 small apple, finely diced
½ cup celery, finely diced
½ cup peanut butter

Mix all ingredients together. Spread on bread slices and top with another slice. Makes 4 to 5 sandwiches.

PEANUT BUTTER-PINEAPPLE SANDWICH FILLING

½ cup chunky peanut butter
1 can (8-oz.) crushed pineapple, well drained

Combine peanut butter and pineapple. Spread between slices of buttered bread. Filling will keep up to 10 days in refrigerator. Sandwiches may also be frozen for future use.

PRONTO SPAGHETTI

½ lb. ground beef
¼ cup chopped green pepper
¼ cup chopped onion
1 can (16-oz.) spaghetti sauce with mushrooms
¼ tsp. dried oregano
¼ cup dry red wine
4 oz. spaghetti, broken up

Cook beef, onion, and green pepper in skillet until meat is browned. Drain off fat. Stir in spaghetti sauce, oregano and wine. Simmer, uncovered, 25 minutes.

Cook spaghetti according to package directions. Drain and rinse. Toss with sauce and spoon desired amount into a wide mouth thermos. Keeps up to 4 days refrigerated.

Kid Pleasers

RAVIOLI SOUP

1 Tbsp. vegetable oil
1/2 cup sliced celery
1/2 cup sliced carrot
1 can chicken broth
Dash pepper
1 can (15-oz.) beef ravioli in sauce

Saute celery and carrots in oil. Add broth, one soup can water and pepper. Bring to boil, then simmer 15 minutes. Stir in ravioli, heat gently to boiling and simmer 5 minutes. Spoon into a wide mouth thermos. Remainder keeps up to 4 days refrigerated. (serves 3)

TACOS

1/4 lb. ground beef
1/4 cup mild taco sauce
1 cup shredded mild cheddar cheese
1/2 cup diced tomatoes
1 cup finely shredded lettuce
2 packaged taco shells

Brown beef in skillet; drain well. Stir in taco sauce and heat thoroughly. Spoon meat mixture into small thermos with a wide mouth. Place cheese, tomatoes and lettuce in separate sandwich bags. Wrap shells in paper napkins and place in sandwich bags (don't forget the plastic spoon for putting it all together).

SIDE DISHES

CANDIED YAMS

    1 small can yams, drained
    ½ cup brown sugar
    2 Tbsp. water
    ½ cup crushed pineapple, drained
    1 Tbsp. margarine, melted
    ¼ tsp. salt

Place all ingredients in skillet. Heat over medium heat, stirring carefully, until yams are heated through. Spoon into a wide mouth thermos. Remaining yams may be refrigerated and reheated later. Keeps up to 6 days.

CARROT-RAISIN SALAD

    2 cups raw grated carrots
    ½ cup seedless raisins
    2 Tbsp. lemon juice
    2 Tbsp. French dressing
    Dash salt

Mix all ingredients. Chill. Pack in small plastic container or cup with tight fitting lid. Keeps up to 5 days.

Kid Pleasers

CHEESY POTATO SALAD

2 cups cooked, diced potatoes
2 hard-cooked eggs, diced
½ tsp. salt
½ cup diced celery
¼ cup diced onion
½ cup cubed cheese
¼ cup minced sweet pickles
¼ cup sweet pickle juice
½ cup mayonnaise
Paprika

Combine potatoes, eggs, salt, celery, onion, cheese and pickles. Mix pickle juice with mayonnaise. Pour over potato mixture and toss. Chill. Keeps up to 6 days.

CINNAMON GELATIN

1 pkg. (3-oz.) cherry flavored gelatin
1 cup boiling water
2 Tbsp. red cinnamon candies
2 cups applesauce
½ cup chopped celery
½ cup chopped walnuts

Dissolve gelatin and candies in water, stirring until candies are completely dissolved. Cool. Add applesauce. When gelatin begins to jell, fold in celery and nuts. Chill thoroughly. Cut into squares. Keeps up to 7 days refrigerated.

CREAM OF TOMATO SOUP

2½ cups tomatoes
⅓ cup chopped onion
3 Tbsp. sugar
1 tsp. salt
½ tsp. monosodium glutamate
½ bay leaf
2 Tbsp. margarine
3 Tbsp. flour
2 cups cold milk

Combine tomatoes, onion, sugar, seasoning and bay leaf in saucepan. Simmer 5 minutes. Discard bay leaf and strain, forcing pulp of tomato through sieve. Make white sauce from margarine, flour and milk. Add hot tomato mixture. Heat thoroughly before pouring into thermos.

MOCK BAKED BEANS

¼ cup catsup
3 Tbsp. minced onion
2 Tbsp. molasses
2 Tbsp. brown sugar
¼ tsp. salt
2 drops hot pepper sauce
1 can (1 lb.) baked beans

Combine all ingredients in saucepan and heat thoroughly. Spoon into a wide mouth thermos. Unused portions keep up to 6 days refrigerated.

Kid Pleasers

NUTS AND BOLTS

½ lb. margarine, melted
2 Tbsp. Worcestershire sauce
1 Tbsp. celery salt
1½ Tbsp. allspice
2 Tbsp. garlic salt
¼ cup vegetable oil
2 Tbsp. monosodium glutamate
1 pkg. slim pretzels
1 qt. shoestring potatoes
1 box square-shaped wheat cereal
1 box square-shaped rice cereal
1 lb. mixed nuts

Combine margarine, Worcestershire, celery salt, allspice, garlic salt, vegetable oil and monosodium glutamate in saucepan and heat over low heat for a few minutes to blend flavors.

Combine remaining ingredients in large bowl and pour warm margarine mixture over. Toss to coat.

Spread a thin layer of snack mixture on cookie sheet. Bake 200°F. for 3 hours. Repeat with remaining mixture.

PINEAPPLE COLESLAW

2 cups finely shredded cabbage
1 cup drained crushed pineapple
3 Tbsp. bottled Russian dressing

Combine all ingredients. Spoon into 4 individual containers; cover and chill. Keeps up to 5 days.

WALDORF SALAD

1 medium-sized apple, cored and diced
1 orange, peeled and diced
1 cup diced celery
½ cup chopped walnuts
¼ cup mayonnaise

Combine ingredients; mix and chill. Spoon into lettuce lined containers with tight fitting lid. Unused salad keeps up to 3 days.

Kid Pleasers 186

CARAMEL POPCORN BALLS

¼ cup margarine
1 cup brown sugar
½ cup corn syrup
½ 15-oz. can sweetened condensed milk
½ tsp. vanilla
5 qts. popped corn

Combine margarine, sugar and syrup. Stir well and bring to boil over medium heat. Stir in milk and simmer, stirring, to 235°F. Remove from heat and stir in vanilla. Pour over popcorn. Shape into balls with buttered hands. Wrap individually in plastic wrap.

CHOCOLATE CHIP COOKIES

½ cup margarine
1 cup sugar
1 egg
¼ tsp. baking soda
2½ cups flour
1 tsp. baking powder
½ tsp. vanilla
½ cup sour cream
1 cup chocolate chips

Cream together shortening and sugar; add egg, slightly beaten. Add soda dissolved in sour cream. Sift together flour and baking powder. Add to creamed mixture and stir to blend well. Fold in chocolate chips. Drop by spoonfuls onto greased cookie sheet. Bake 350°F. 15 to 20 minutes.

Kid Pleasers

CHOCOLATE DOUGHNUTS

1/4 cup margarine
1 1/2 cups sugar
2 eggs, well beaten
1 1/2 sq. melted chocolate
1 cup buttermilk
4 cups flour
1 tsp. baking soda
1 tsp. cinnamon
Dash salt
1 1/2 tsp. vanilla

Cream margarine and sugar, then beat until fluffy; add eggs, chocolate and sour milk. Sift together dry ingredients. Stir, a little at a time, into mixture, beating vigorously. Add vanilla and enough flour to handle mixture. Toss onto a lightly floured cloth. Knead a few minutes before rolling to 1/4" thickness. Dip doughnut cutter into flour, then cut out shape from dough. Deep fry until done and drain on paper towels.

GINGERBREAD CUPCAKES

1/2 cup shortening
1/2 cup sugar
1/2 cup molasses
2 eggs
1/2 tsp. baking soda
1/2 cup cold water
1 1/2 cups flour
1 tsp. baking powder
1 tsp. ginger
1 tsp. cinnamon
1 cup shredded coconut

Cream together shortening and sugar. Add molasses and egg; beat smooth. Dissolve soda in cold water and add to mixture. Add flour, baking powder, spices and salt, then fold in coconut. Spoon into muffin pans with paper liners. Bake at 350°F. 25 minutes. May be frosted with vanilla icing or left plain. Freezes well.

Kid Pleasers

MACAROONS

2 egg whites
1 cup sugar
1 cup shredded coconut
1/2 cup chopped walnuts
2 cups corn flakes
1 tsp. vanilla
1 Tbsp. flour

Beat egg whites; add sugar, coconut, nuts, corn flakes and vanilla. Mix well, then add flour all at once. Stir to form a firm dough. Drop by spoonfuls onto a greased cookie sheet. Bake 300°F. 15 to 20 minutes.

ORANGE CANDY

1 cup sugar
1 1/2 cups sweetened condensed milk
2 cups sugar
Grated rind of 2 oranges
1/2 cup butter
1 cup pecans

Melt 1 cup sugar in large kettle. Scald milk in top of double boiler. When sugar has melted to a rich yellow, add the hot milk all at once, stirring. Add 2 cups of sugar and stir until dissolved. Cook to 238°F. Remove from heat and add rind, butter and nuts. Beat until creamy. Pour onto buttered platter to cool. Cut into squares and wrap each separately in plastic wrap.

PEANUT BUTTER COOKIES

1 cup chunky peanut butter
1 cup sugar
1 egg
1/2 tsp. vanilla extract

Mix peanut butter and sugar, then stir in egg and vanilla. Shape into 1" balls and put on ungreased cookie sheets. Press with fork to flatten. Bake 350°F. 12 to 15 minutes.

Kid Pleasers

TAFFY APPLES

6 medium-sized apples
6 wooden skewers
1 cup sugar
1 cup brown sugar
½ cup water
½ cup vinegar

Stick skewer into core of each apple. Make syrup by boiling together sugars, water and vinegar. Cook mixture until it reaches the soft craft stage. Dip apples in syrup, making certain they are evenly coated. Place, blossom side down, on waxed paper to dry. Wrap each lightly with plastic wrap.

Chapter 10

Totable Beverages

COLD BEVERAGES

AMBROSIA

> *Juice of 4 oranges*
> *Juice of 1 grapefruit*
> *½ cup sugar*
> *½ cup water*

Dissolve sugar in water; add to juices. Chill. Pour into thermos and add 6 ice cubes (the ice cubes will dilute the mixture and keep it properly chilled.)

CHERRYADE

> *1 can (6-oz.) frozen lemonade concentrate,*
> *thawed*
> *2 cans ice water*
> *2 cups cherry juice*

Combine all ingredients and pour into chilled thermos.

CHERRY TEA

1 cup water
½ cup sugar
1 cup double-strength tea
1 cup fresh pie cherries, pitted
¾ cup cherry juice
½ cup lemon juice
1 quart water

Put 1 cup water and sugar in saucepan and bring to boil. Boil 5 minutes. Cool. Combine remaining ingredients in blender container and blend until cherries are liquified. Add sugar syrup and remaining water. Chill. Pour into chilled thermos. Shake thermos before serving.

CINNAMON ICED COFFEE

3½ cups hot strong coffee
6 inches stick cinnamon
½ cup whipping cream
2 tsp. sugar

Pour hot coffee over stick cinnamon. Add cream; chill. Pour into chilled thermos.

COFFEE EGGNOG

2 eggs, separated
½ cup sugar
2 Tbsp. instant coffee powder
2 cups milk
½ cup heavy cream
1 tsp. vanilla extract
Dash of nutmeg

Beat egg yolks. Gradually add ¼ cup sugar, beating until fluffy. Dissolve coffee in 3 Tbsp. water, stir in milk, cream, and vanilla. Chill. Beat egg whites stiff, gradually add remaining sugar. Fold into egg yolk mixture. Pour into chilled thermos. Shake before drinking.

CRANBERRY COOLER

1 quart cranberry-apple juice, chilled
1/2 Tbsp. rum flavoring
2 Tbsp. honey
8 ice cubes

Whirl all ingredients in blender container; pour into chilled thermos.

CRANBERRY-GRAPE JUICE

1 bottle (32-oz.) cranberry juice cocktail
1 1/2 cups grape juice

Combine juices and chill thoroughly before pouring into thermos.

FIRECRACKER PUNCH

2 cups cranberry juice cocktail
1 can (16-oz.) frozen lemonade concentrate
1/2 cup sweet vermouth
1 cup water

Combine all ingredients in blender. Blend at high speed 30 seconds. Chill before pouring into thermos.

FRESH APPLE DRINK

1 cup water
2 Tbsp. lemon juice
2 tsp. sugar
2 tart apples, peeled, cored, and grated
1 cup crushed ice

Put water, sugar, lemon juice, and apples in blender and blend until smooth. Add ice and blend at high speed until ice is liquefied. Pour into chilled thermos.

FRESH STRAWBERRY LIMEADE

$\frac{1}{2}$ cup lime juice
3 cups cold water
$\frac{1}{4}$ cup sugar
3 cups sliced strawberries

Place all ingredients in blender and liquefy. Chill before pouring into thermos.

FRUIT PUNCH

1 quart cold water
2 cups sugar
$\frac{1}{2}$ cup lemon juice
1 cup pineapple juice
1 cup apricot nectar
1 cup orange juice

Boil water and sugar. Cool. Add fruit juice. Chill and pour into the thermos.

GUAVA-MILK PUNCH

1 can (12-oz. guava nectar)
1 egg
$\frac{1}{2}$ cup milk
2 Tbsp. freshly squeezed lemon juice

Put all ingredients in blender container and blend well. Chill. Pour into thermos and shake well before serving.

LEMONADE

1 cup sugar
1 cup water
6 Tbsp. lemon juice, (freshly squeezed)
4 cups water

Combine sugar and water in saucepan. Heat to a full boil. Cool, add lemon juices and water. Chill. Pour into thermos.

Totable Beverages 194

MINT LEMONADE

5 lemons
½ cup freshly crushed mint leaves
2 cups sugar
2 quarts water

Extract juice from lemons and add to the crushed mint leaves. Add sugar and water; bring to boil, remove from heat and allow to cool. Strain. Chill thoroughly.

MINT LIMEADE

1 cup fresh mint leaves
1 cup sugar
1 cup boiling water
1½ quarts cold water
1¼ cup freshly squeezed lime juice
Few drops of green food coloring

Put mint, sugar, and boiling water in blender container and run on high speed until mint is chopped. Cool; strain. Add cold water, lime juice, and food coloring. Chill before adding to thermos.

ORANGEADE

1 cup orange juice
1 cup carbonated water
2 Tbsp. lemon juice
2 Tbsp. sugar

Dissolve sugar in orange juice. Add lemon juice and mix well. Pour into thermos. Add carbonated water, stir quickly and close thermos.

ORANGE-CRANBERRY JUICE

$1/4$ cup sugar
1 $3/4$ cups water
1 can (6-oz.) frozen concentrated orange juice
2 cups cranberry juice cocktail
2 Tbsp. lemon juice

Mix sugar and water in saucepan. Bring to a boil, stirring until sugar is dissolved. Remove from heat and stir in remaining ingredients. Chill before pouring into thermos.

ORANGE-PAPAYA WOO JUICE

3 cups orange juice
2 cups papaya juice
2 Tbsp. powdered milk

Combine ingredients in blender and blend until thoroughly mixed. Pour into chilled thermos. Shake before pouring.

PAPAYA-BANANA SHAKE-UP

2 cups papaya juice
2 cups milk
2 ripe bananas, peeled
8 ice cubes

Blend all in blender container and pour into chilled thermos.

PINEAPPLE-CARROT COCKTAIL

2 cups pineapple juice
3 medium carrots, peeled and shredded
1 small banana, peeled and mashed
$2/3$ cup cold water

Put all ingredients in blender container and liquefy. Chill before pouring into thermos.

Totable Beverages   196

PINEAPPLE-LEMONADE

1 pint water
1 cup sugar
1 cup grated pineapple
Juice of 3 lemons
1 quart ice water

Make syrup by boiling water and sugar 10 minutes; add pineapple and lemon juice. Cool; strain. Add ice water. Pour into chilled thermos.

PINK WINE BLOSSOM

1 can (12-oz.) frozen lemonade concentrate
3 cups rose'
12 ice cubes
12 sliced strawberries (optional)

Combine all ingredients in blender. Whirl until forthy and ice is crushed. Pour into chilled thermos.

ROSE' FRAPPE'

½ fifth rose'
½ (6-oz.) can frozen lemonade concentrate
½ cup water
8 ice cubes

Whirl all in blender container until ice is crushed. Pour into chilled thermos.

Totable Beverages

SPICED ICED COFFEE

2 Tbsp. instant coffee
4 cups hot water
2 Tbsp. sugar
2 cinnamon sticks
6 whole cloves
6 whole allspice

Dissolve coffee in hot water. Pour over sugar and spices in saucepan. Cover and let steep 1 hour. Strain and chill spiced coffee before pouring into thermos.

TEA LEMONADE

1 Tbsp. mint jelly
½ quart hot tea
½ can (6-oz.) frozen lemonade, reconstituted

Dissolve jelly in tea. Mix with lemonade and chill thoroughly before pouring into thermos.

TEA NOG

2 eggs, separated
½ cup sugar
3 Tbsp. instant tea
3 cups milk

Beat egg whites stiff, then gradually add sugar. Combine egg yolks with tea with milk. Beat well. Slowly stir tea mixture into egg whites. Pour into chilled thermos.

TEA PUNCH

1 cup pineapple juice
1 cup fresh strawberries, sliced
1 can (6-oz.) frozen lemonade concentrate, thawed
3 Tbsp. instant tea
3 cups water

Put all ingredients in blender container and liquefy. Chill before filling thermos.

Totable Beverages 198

TEA SPARKLE

1 cup boiling water
4 tea bags
1 cup light corn syrup
4 cups cold water
½ cup lime juice
½ cup orange juice

Pour boiling water over tea bags, steep 5 minutes; strain. Add corn syrup, cold water, and juices. Mix thoroughly. Chill. Pour into thermos.

TOMATO JUICE COCKTAIL

1½ cups tomato juice
½ cup evaporated milk
½ tsp. celery salt
Dash pepper
½ cup water

Mix all ingredients together, chill and pour into chilled thermos.

TROPICAL ICED TEA

2 cups boiling water
2 tea bags
¼ cup sugar
4 limes
2 cups unsweetened pineapple juise
1 can ginger ale

Pour water over tea bags in a ½ gallon container. Let steep 3 to 5 minutes. Discard bags. Stir in sugar. Squeeze lime and add juice to tea. Add pineapple juice; stir well. Chill. Pour tea into thermos, along with a few ice cubes. Pack can of ginger ale with lunch. Add ginger ale just before serving.

Totable Beverages

HOT BEVERAGES

APPLE-HONEY TEA

1 can (6-oz.) frozen apple cider concentrate
1 Tbsp. instant tea
½ Tbsp. honey
¼ tsp. cinnamon

Reconstitute apple cider concentrate according to can directions. Add tea, honey, and cinnamon. Pour into saucepan and heat through. Pour into thermos. Shake thermos before serving.

CAFE' CUBA

¼ cup instant coffee powder
¼ cup water
¼ cup dark brown sugar
3 cups milk

Combine all ingredients and heat slowly in saucepan. Do not boil. Pour into thermos. Shake thermos before pouring.

CRANBERRY-APPLE TEA

2 cups cranberry juice cocktail
2 cups apple juice
3 Tbsp. instant tea
2 stick cinnamon
10 whole cloves

Combine cranberry and apple juice in saucepan. Add tea and spices; bring to a boil, then reduce heat and simmer 5 to 10 minutes. Strain. May be served hot or chilled.

Totable Beverages

HONEY COFFEE

4 Tbsp. honey
2 cups hot double-strength coffee
2 cups warm milk

Stir honey into coffee. Add to saucepan along with warm milk. Heat for a few minutes, stirring (do not boil). Pour into thermos.

HOT COCOA

1/4 cup cocoa
1/3 cup sugar
1/2 cup water
1 quart milk
1/2 tsp. vanilla
Marshmallows

Combine cocoa, sugar and water in saucepan and heat over medium heat 5 to 7 minutes. Add milk and heat over low heat until scalded. Add vanilla and pour into thermos. Wrap marshmallows in plastic wrap until cocoa is served. Float marshmallows in cup of cocoa.

HOT MOCHA

5 cups milk
1/4 cup instant coffee
1/2 cup chocolate syrup

Heat milk over medium heat 5 minutes. Do not allow to boil. Stir in instant coffee and chocolate syrup; continue to heat, stirring until coffee is dissolved. Immediately pour into thermos.

HOT SPICED CIDER

½ gallon cider
½ Tbsp. whole cloves
3 Tbsp. brown sugar
2 Tbsp. stick cinnamon

Heat cider in large saucepan. Add sugar; stir to dissolve. Tie cloves and cinnamon in a square of cheesecloth and add bundle to cider. Allow to simmer 10 to 12 minutes. Remove spices and pour into thermos. Remainder may be stored in the refrigerator and reheated later.

HOT SPICED COFFEE

4 cups water
2 Tbsp. instant coffee
½ tsp. whole allspice
Peel of 1 orange
1 cinnamon stick

Combine all ingredients, except cinnamon, in saucepan; heat to boiling. Strain mixture and pour into thermos; add cinnamon stick.

HOT SPICED TEA

½ cup sugar
Juice of 1 orange
Juice of ½ lemon
1 tea bag
4 cups hot water
6 whole cloves
1 cinnamon stick

Mix sugar with orange and lemon juices; pour into hot water in saucepan. Add tea bag and spices. Cover and let steep 20 minutes. Strain. Reheat and pour into thermos. Shake before serving.

Totable Beverages

HOT TOMATO BOUILLON

2 cups tomato juice
1 can (10½-oz.) condensed beef broth
2 tsp. lemon juice
½ tsp. Worcestershire sauce
¼ tsp. horseradish

Combine ingredients in saucepan. Heat to boiling and pour into thermos.

LEMON BROTH

1 can (10½-oz.) condensed chicken broth
1 cup water
3 Tbsp. lemon juice

Combine ingredients in saucepan and heat to boiling. Pour into thermos and float a couple of lemon slices on top.

MEXICAN CHOCOLATE

½ quart milk
1 inch of stick cinnamon
1 Tbsp. instant coffee
1 square of sweet chocolate
¼ cup boiling water
½ tsp. vanilla.

Heat milk to scalding with cinnamon stick and coffee. Dissolve chocolate in boiling water and add to milk. Heat again to boiling point; remove from heat and add vanilla. Discard cinnamon. Pour into thermos. Shake well before serving.

MULLED GRAPE JUICE

1 can frozen grape juice
3 cans water
2¹/₂ sticks cinnamon.
2 tsp. cloves

Combine juice and water in saucepan. Tie spices in bag and add to juice. Simmer gently for 10 minutes. Remove spices and pour juice into thermos.

MULLED TOMATO JUICE

4 cups tomato juice
¹/₂ tsp. Worcestershire sauce
¹/₂ tsp. celery salt
¹/₄ tsp. oregano
1 drop hot pepper sauce

Combine ingredients in saucepan and heat to boiling. Pour into thermos.

MULLED WINE

¹/₂ cup sugar
1¹/₂ cups water
1 Tbsp. grated lemon peel
9 whole cloves
1 bottle (4/5 quart) red dinner wine

Boil together sugar, water, lemon peel, and cloves. Add wine and heat gently. Strain and pour into thermos.

ORANGE COFFEE

4 cups strong black coffee
1 cup fresh orange juice
¹/₂ tsp. grated orange rind
1¹/₂ Tbsp. light-brown sugar

Combine all ingredients in saucepan. Heat thoroughly, pour into thermos.

Totable Beverages

RUBY RED CONSOMME'

1 can condensed consomme'
1 cup tomato juice
½ cup water
Combine ingredients. Heat thoroughly. Serve hot or chilled.

SPICED LEMONADE

4 whole cloves
1 stick cinnamon
1 cup cranberry juice
2 cups water
½ can (6-oz.) frozen lemonade concentrate
Mix spices, cranberry juice, and water in saucepan. Bring to boil. Cover; remove from heat and let stand 10 minutes. Strain and discard spices. Add lemonade and reheat. Pour into thermos.

Totable Beverages   **206**

Chapter 11

Sweet Finales

QUICK DESSERT BREADS AND MUFFINS

APPLE BREAD

2 cups flour
1 tsp. salt
1 tsp. baking powder
1 tsp. cinnamon
½ tsp. baking soda
½ tsp. nutmeg
¼ tsp. cloves
½ cup margarine
¾ cup brown sugar
2 eggs
1 cup grated apple
¼ cup buttermilk
½ cup walnuts

Mix together margarine, sugar, eggs, apple, and milk. Add sifted dry ingredients. Stir in walnuts. Pour into greased pan. Bake 350°F. 55 to 60 minutes. Cool completely before slicing.

BANANA BREAD

1 cup sugar
½ cup margarine
2 eggs
2 cups flour
1 tsp. baking soda
3 mashed ripe bananas
1 cup broken walnuts

Combine sugar, margarine, and eggs. Mix well. Add flour and soda. Mix before stirring in bananas and walnuts. Pour into greased loaf pan. Bake 375°F. 45 minutes.

CARROT BREAD

¾ cup oil
1 cup sugar
2 eggs, beaten
¼ tsp. salt
1 cup raw carrots, shredded
1½ cup flour
1 tsp. cinnamon
1 tsp. baking soda
½ cup nuts
1 tsp. vanilla

Mix together salad oil, sugar, and eggs. Sift dry ingredients and add to oil mixture. Pour into greased, floured bread pan. Bake 1½ hours at 350°F. Cool before slicing.

CRANBERRY BREAD

2 cups flour
¾ cup sugar
1½ tsp. baking powder
½ tsp. baking soda
¼ tsp. salt
1 egg
3 Tbsp. grated orange rind
½ cup fresh orange juice
3 Tbsp. melted margarine
2 Tbsp. hot water
1½ cups cranberries, halved
1 cup chopped walnuts

Sift together dry ingredients. Beat together egg, orange rind, juice, margarine, and hot water. Add dry ingredients and mix well. Fold in cranberries and nuts. Turn batter into well greased and floured 9 x 5 x 3" loaf pan. Bake 350°F. 55 to 60 minutes. Remove from pan and cool on wire rack. Cool completely before slicing.

PUMPKIN-NUT BREAD

2 cups sugar
1 egg
½ cup salad oil
1 tsp. salt
2 tsp. baking soda
2½ cups flour
½ tsp. cloves
½ tsp. cinnamon
2 cups canned pumpkin
⅔ cup raisins
1 cup chopped walnuts

Sift dry ingredients. Blend sugar, egg, and oil in large bowl; mix well. Add to dry ingredients, alternately with pumpkin. Fold in raisins and nuts. Bake in well greased loaf pan at 325°F. 1 hour. Cool before slicing.

Sweet Finales

RAISIN BRAN MUFFINS

   3/4 cup boiling water
   1 cup 100% bran cereal
   1 egg
   1/2 cup salad oil
   1 cup unflavored yogurt
   1/2 cup sorgum
   1/2 cup brown sugar
   2 cups 40% bran flakes
   1/2 cup chopped walnuts
   1 cup raisins
   1 cup unprocessed bran
   1 1/2 cups whole wheat flour
   2 tsp. baking soda
   1/4 tsp. salt

   Combine boiling water and 100% bran. Let cool. Add next 8 ingredients and mix well.

   Sift together remaining ingredients. Add to batter and stir until just moistened. Spoon into muffin tins lined with paper muffin cups, filling 3/4 full. Bake in 375°F. oven approximately 30 minutes. Makes 2 dozen. Freezes well.

ZUCCHINI BREAD

   2 eggs, well beaten
   1 cup vegetable oil
   2 cups sugar
   2 cups grated zucchini
   3 Tbsp. grated orange rind
   1 Tbsp. vanilla extract
   3 cups sifted flour
   1/2 tsp. salt
   1/4 tsp. baking powder
   1 tsp. baking soda
   3/4 tsp. nutmeg
   1 Tbsp. cinnamon
   1 cup walnuts

   Grate unpeeled zucchini. Add eggs, oil, sugar, rind, and vanilla. Mix dry ingredients and add to egg mixture. Mix well and add nuts. Grease and flour 2 loaf pans. Bake 350°F. 1 hour. Cool completely before slicing. Freezes well.

Sweet Finales

APPLESAUCE CUPCAKES

4 cups flour
2 cups sugar
1 tsp. nutmeg
½ tsp. cloves
½ tsp. allspice
⅔ cup margarine
½ cup warm water
2 Tbsp. cocoa
1½ tsp. baking powder
1 cup raisins
1 cup walnuts or pecans
2 cups applesauce
2 tsp. baking soda

Sift dry ingredients several times. Add soda to applesauce. Combine sifted dry ingredients, water, and applesauce into a bowl. Beat well. Add raisins and nuts. Spoon into paper-lined muffin tins. Bake 350°F. 30 minutes. Cupcakes freeze well.

EASY DATE CRUMB CAKE

1 package (14-oz.) date bar mix
2 cups packaged biscuit mix
3 Tbsp. sugar
⅔ cup milk
1 egg, slightly beaten
2 Tbsp. vegetable oil

Prepare date filling and crumb mixture according to package directions. Pat 1½ cups of the crumb mixture into bottom of ungreased 9 x 9 x 2" pan. Combine biscuit mix and sugar. Blend milk, egg, and oil; stir into dry ingredients until well mixed. Spread half of the biscuit mixture over crumbs in pan. Top with date filling; spreading remaining biscuit mixture carefully over filling. Sprinkle with remaining crumb mixture. Bake 375°F. for 30 minutes. Cool and cut into squares.

211   **Sweet Finales**

FRESH ORANGE CAKE

3 cups sifted cake flour
1 Tbsp. baking powder
1/2 tsp. salt
3/4 cup soft margarine
1 1/2 cups sugar
3 eggs
1 Tbsp. grated orange rind
1/2 cup freshly squeezed orange juice
2/3 cup milk

Glaze:
1 Tbsp. melted margarine
1 Tbsp. milk
1 Tbsp. orange juice
1 tsp. grated orange rind
1 cup confectioner's sugar

Grease 2 9x1½" layer cake pans; dust lightly with flour. Sift together flour, baking powder, and salt. Combine shortening, sugar, eggs, and rind; beat well. Stir into flour mixture alternately with orange juice and milk; beating well after each addition until batter is smooth. Pour batter into prepared pans. Bake at 350°F. 30 to 35 minutes.

Combine glaze ingredients and beat until smooth. Spread between cooled cake layers. Cut into wedges and wrap individually. Unused portions may be frozen for later use.

FRUIT COCKTAIL CAKE

1 cup sugar
1 cup flour
1 tsp. baking soda
½ tsp. salt
2 cups drained fruit cocktail
½ cup fruit cocktail syrup
1 egg
1 cup brown sugar
½ cup chopped walnuts

Mix sugar, flour, soda, and salt. Add fruit cocktail, syrup, and egg. Beat well. Spoon batter into greased and floured 8 x 8" pan and sprinkle with brown sugar and nuts. Bake at 300°F. 50 minutes. Cool before cutting into squares.

GRAHAM CRACKER CAKE

1 cup sugar
2 Tbsp. melted margarine
2 eggs, separated
1 cup milk
1 cup rolled graham crackers
1 cup flour
2 tsp. baking powder
1 cup chopped walnuts

Cream sugar, margarine, and egg yolks. Stir in milk, cracker crumbs, flour, and baking powder. Beat egg whites until stiff. Fold into batter along with nuts. Spoon into greased and floured loaf pan and bake at 350°F. 45 to 50 minutes. Cool before slicing. Freezes well.

Sweet Finales

MAYONNAISE CAKE

4 Tbsp. cocoa
Pinch of salt
2 cups flour
1 cup sugar
2 tsp. baking soda
1 cup milk
1 cup mayonnaise
1 tsp. vanilla

Grease 8" square pan. Mix dry ingredients in large bowl. Gradually add milk. Fold in mayonnaise; add vanilla. Pour into pan and bake 30 minutes at 350°F. Cut into squares when cool. Freezes well.

QUICK AND EASY LOAFER'S CAKE

1 can pie filling (cherry, raisin, apple, blueberry, etc.)
1 small package white cake mix (single layer)
⅔ cup oatmeal
½ cup margarine, melted
⅔ cup walnuts, chopped

Grease 8" square pan and pour in pie filling. Combine cake mix and oatmeal, then sprinkle over filling. Dribble with melted margarine. Top with nuts. Bake at 350°F. for 40 minutes. Cool and cut into squares. Spoon into individual serving containers.

RHUBARB CRUMB CAKE

1/2 cup margarine
1 1/2 cups packed brown sugar
1 egg
1 tsp. baking soda
1 cup buttermilk
2 cups flour
1 1/2 cups cut up rhubarb
1 tsp. vanilla
1/2 cup chopped nuts
1/2 cup sugar
1 tsp. cinnamon
1 Tbsp. margarine
2/3 cup chopped walnuts

Cream together margarine and brown sugar. Add egg and blend well. Combine soda and buttermilk, then add alternately with flour. Stir in rhubarb, nuts, and vanilla. Pat into greased 9 x 13" baking dish. Combine sugar, cinnamon, margarine, and nuts. Sprinkle over rhubarb mixture and bake at 350°F. 30 to 40 minutes. Cool. Cut into squares.

TOMATO SOUP CAKE

1 1/2 cups sugar
1/2 cup shortening
2 eggs
2 cups flour
2 tsp. baking powder
1 tsp. baking soda
1 1/2 tsp. cinnamon
1/2 tsp. nutmeg
1 tsp. cloves
1 can tomato soup
1/2 can cold water
1 cup chopped walnuts
2/3 cup raisins

Cream shortening and sugar. Dissolve soda in soup and add to mixture. Add eggs and water; mix well. Add flour, spices, nuts, and raisins. Pour into 8 x 8" loaf pan. Bake 325°F. 1 hour. Cool before cutting into squares.

Sweet Finales

DATE PIE

2 cups milk
1/3 lb. pitted dates
2 eggs, beaten
Dash salt
Dash nutmeg
1 unbaked pie shell

Cook dates with milk twenty minutes in top of double boiler. Cool slightly, then puree in blender. Add remaining ingredients and mix well. Pour into pie shell. Bake 400°F. 10 minutes then reduce heat to 350°F. and bake 25 to 30 minutes longer. Cool. Cut into wedges and pack in wedge-shaped containers.

SOUTHERN PECAN PIE

3/4 cup pecans, chopped fine
1 unbaked pie shell
4 eggs
1/2 cup sugar
1/4 tsp. salt
1 1/4 cups dark corn syrup
1/2 cup margarine, melted
1 tsp. vanilla

Sprinkle nuts into pastry shell. Beat eggs slightly; then beat in remaining ingredients. Pour into pastry shell. Bake at 350°F. 45 minutes, or until center is almost set but still soft. Cool completely before cutting. Pack in wedge-shaped containers.

RAISIN TARTS

1 egg, beaten
1/2 cup brown sugar
1 1/4 cup raisins
3/4 cup chopped walnuts
1 tsp. vanilla
6 small unbaked tart shells

Beat together egg and sugar. Add raisins, nuts, and vanilla. Spoon into tart shells. Bake 400°F. 20 minutes. Cool.

Sweet Finales **216**

DROP COOKIES, BARS, AND SQUARES

CHICKEN BONES

1 cup soft margarine
1/2 cup crunchy peanut butter
2 1/2 cups powdered sugar
1 tsp. vanilla
2 cups graham cracker crumbs
1 cup coconut
2 cups chocolate chips
1/2 cup grated parafin

Combine margarine, peanut butter, powdered sugar, vanilla, crumbs, and coconut. Mix well. Shape into 2" fingers. Place on waxed paper and chill. Over hot water, melt chips and parafin. Dip cookies in chocolate to cover. Place on waxed paper lined cookie sheet and chill.

HAYSTACKS

1 pkg. (6-oz.) butterscotch chips
2 tsp. salad oil
2 cups chow mein noodles
2 cups minature marshmallows

Melt butterscotch in double boiler over hot water. Stir in oil. Mix chow mein noodles and marshmallows in bowl; pour on butterscotch and mix thoroughly with fork. Drop by spoonfuls onto waxed paper and allow to set.

Sweet Finales

NO-BAKE MISSOURI COOKIES

6 Tbsp. cocoa
2 cups sugar
1/2 cup margarine
1/2 cup milk
3/4 cup peanut butter
1 tsp. vanilla
1 1/2 cups coconut
4 cups quick-cooking rolled oats

Mix cocoa and sugar together in saucepan. Add margarine and milk. Bring to boil 1 minute. Remove from heat. Add peanut butter, vanilla, coconut, and oats. Stir well. Drop by spoonfuls onto waxed paper and allow to harden.

OATMEAL MACAROONS

1 cup margarine
1 cup sugar
2 eggs
1 cup brown sugar
1/2 tsp. vanilla
1 1/4 cup flour
1 tsp. baking soda
1/2 tsp. salt
1/2 tsp. cinnamon
3 cups rolled oats
1 pkg. (6-oz.) chocolate chips

Cream together margarine and sugars. Add eggs and vanilla. Sift together dry ingredients and add to creamed mixture. Fold in oats and chocolate chips. Bake on ungreased cookie sheet at 350°F. for 10 to 12 minutes.

RAISIN-OATMEAL COOKIES

1 pkg. yellow cake mix (2 layer size)
2 cups quick-cooking rolled oats
¼ tsp. salt
1 tsp. cinnamon
½ tsp. nutmeg
1 can (22-oz.) raisin pie filling
2 eggs
¼ cup vegetable oil
1 cup walnuts, chopped

Combine all ingredients, except nuts. Beat until blended. Stir in nuts. Drop from spoon onto greased cookie sheet. Bake at 350°F. 15 to 17 minutes. Freezes well.

SOFT MOLASSES COOKIES

2½ cups sifted flour
2 tsp. baking soda
1 tsp. ground ginger
1 tsp. ground cinnamon
Dash salt
½ cup softened margarine
½ cup sugar
½ cup molasses
1 egg
¼ cup cold water
1 cup raisins

Heat oven to 375°F. Sift flour, soda, spices, and salt together. Cream together, margarine, sugar, molasses, and eggs. Add sifted ingredients alternately with cold water; beat until blended. Stir in raisins. Drop by rounded teaspoonfuls about 2" apart on lightly greased cookie sheets. Bake 10 to 12 minutes. Cool.

BLOND BROWNIES

1 cup sifted flour
1/2 tsp. baking powder
1/8 tsp. baking soda
1/4 tsp. salt
1/2 cup chopped nuts
1/3 cup margarine
3/4 cup brown sugar
1 egg, slightly beaten
1 tsp. vanilla
1 cup (6-oz.) butterscotch bits

Sift togerher flour, baking powder, soda, and salt. Add nuts and mix well. Set aside.

Melt margarine in saucepan; remove from heat. Add sugar and mix well. Cool slightly. Add eggs and vanilla; blend. Add flour mixture, a small amount at a time, mixing well after each addition. Mix in chips and spread in greased 9 x 9 x 2" pan. Bake at 350°F. for 20 to 25 minutes. Cool in pan before cutting.

BROWNIES

2/3 cup sifted flour
1/2 tsp. baking powder
1/4 tsp. salt
1/3 cup margarine
2 squares unsweetened chocolate
1 cup sugar
2 eggs, well beaten
1 cup chopped walnuts
1 tsp. vanilla

Sift together flour, baking powder, and salt. Melt margarine and chocolate over hot water. Gradually add sugar to beaten eggs, then add chocolate mixture and blend. Add flour and mix well. Stir in nuts and vanilla.

Bake in greased 8" square pan at 350°F. for 25 minutes.

CHERRY FUDGE SQUARES

1 pkg. (regular size) fudge brownie mix
1 egg
3 Tbsp. water
2 Tbsp. maraschino cherry juice
½ cup chopped pecans
½ cup chopped maraschino cherries
1 cup powdered sugar

Combine mix with egg, water, 1 Tbsp. cherry juice, beat well. Stir in nuts and cherries. Spread in greased 9 x 9 x 2" pan. Bake at 350°F. 30 minutes. Cool completely.

Blend powdered sugar and remaining 1 Tbsp. cherry juice until smooth; spread over cookies. Let stand until frosting is firm. Cut into squares. Freezes well.

COCONUT BROWNIES

2 squares unsweetened chocolate
Margarine
2 eggs
Sugar
⅔ cup flour
½ tsp. baking powder
Dash salt
1 tsp. vanilla extract
1 can (3½-oz.) flaked coconut

Melt chocolate and ⅓ cup margarine over low heat. Beat eggs until foamy. Gradually add 1 cup sugar and beat until well blended. Add chocolate-margarine mixture and beat well. Stir in next 4 ingredients and ⅔ cup coconut. Spread in greased 8" square pan. Melt 2 Tbsp. margarine and add 1 Tbsp. sugar and remaining coconut. Mix well and spread evenly on batter in pan. Bake at 350°F. 30 minutes. Cool; then cut into sauares.

Sweet Finales

COFFEE SQUARES

1/2 cup softened margarine
1 cup packed brown sugar
1 egg
1 1/2 cups flour
1/2 tsp. baking powder
1/2 tsp. baking soda
1/2 tsp. cinnamon
Dash salt
1/2 cup hot coffee
1/2 cup chopped walnuts

Cream together margarine and sugar. Beat in egg. Add sifted dry ingredients alternately with coffee, beating after each addition. Add nuts and spread in greased 15 x 10 x 1" pan. Bake 350°F. 15 to 20 minutes. Cool; cut into squares.

FRUIT AND SOUR CREAM SQUARES

1 pkg. sugar cookie mix
1 can (3 1/2-oz.) flaked coconut
1/2 cup raisins
1 egg
1/2 cup sour cream
1/2 tsp. lemon juice

Combine cookie mix, coconut, and raisins. Beat egg and stir in sour cream and lemon extract. Stir into cookie mixture until well blended. Spread into greased 8" square baking pan. Bake 350°F. 35 minutes. Cool completely before cutting into squares. Squares can be wrapped separately and frozen.

GINGERBREAD

1 cup molasses
1/2 cup boiling water
2 1/2 cups flour
1 tsp. baking soda
1 1/2 tsp. ground ginger
1/2 tsp. salt
1/4 cup melted margarine

Add water to molasses. Mix and sift dry ingredients, then combine with water-molasses mixture. Add margarine and beat vigorously. Pour into buttered shallow pan and bake at 350°F. 30 to 35 minutes.

LAYER BAR COOKIES

1/2 cup margarine
1 cup graham cracker crumbs
1 cup semi-sweet chocolate chips
1 cup butterscotch chips
1 1/2 cup flaked coconut
1/2 cup walnuts, chopped
1 1/3 cups sweetened condensed milk

Melt margarine in a 13 x 9 x 2" pan. Sprinkle crumbs evenly over margarine. Layer chocolate, butterscotch, coconut, and nuts on top. Pour condensed milk over all. Bake 350°F. 30 minutes; cool. Cut into bars.

Sweet Finales

LEMON FIG BARS

  ½ cup margarine
  1½ cups firmly packed brown sugar
  2 eggs
  1 tsp. vanilla
  2 cups sifted flour
  1 tsp. baking powder
  1 cup chopped dried figs
  ½ cup chopped walnuts
  1 Tbsp. melted margarine
  1 Tbsp. milk
  1 Tbsp. lemon juice
  1 cup powdered sugar

Cream margarine with brown sugar; beat in eggs and vanilla. Sift in flour, baking powder; stir until well blended. Fold in figs and nuts. Spread in greased 13 x 9 x 2" baking pan. Bake 350°F. 35 minutes.

Combine remaining ingredients and beat smooth. Drizzle over top. Cool completely before cutting into bars.

LEMON SQUARES

Crust:
  ½ cup margarine, softened
  ½ tsp. baking soda
  1 cup flour
  ½ cup firmly packed brown sugar
  ½ cup sugar
  20 saltine crackers, crushed
  ½ cup coconut
Filling:
  2 eggs
  1 cup sugar
  ¼ cup lemon juice
  1 Tbsp. grated lemon peel
  2 Tbsp. water

Blend margarine into baking powder and flour. Add sugars, cracker crumbs, and coconut; mix well. Remove ¾ cup and reserve. Press remaining crumbs into ungreased 9 x 13" pan.

Mix filling ingredients together. Cook in saucepan until mixture thickens. Cool slightly and pour on top of unbaked crust. Sprinkle reserved crumbs on top. Bake at 350°F. for 30 minutes.

WALNUT CHEWS

2 Tbsp. butter
2 eggs
1 cup brown sugar, packed
⅛ tsp. baking soda
1½ cups chopped walnuts
1 tsp. vanilla
¼ cup flour

Melt butter in bottom of 8" square baking pan. Tilt to coat bottom. Beat eggs. Stir together remaining ingredients, then add to eggs; mix well. Pour batter over melted butter and carefully spread evenly (do not stir). Bake 350°F. 20 to 25 minutes. Let chews cool completely in pan. Cut into 2" squares.

FRUITS AND PUDDINGS

APPLE CRISP

4 cups sliced, pared and cored tart apples
1 cup sifted flour
¾ cup packed brown sugar
1 tsp. ground cinnamon
¼ tsp. ground nutmeg
Dash salt
½ cup margarine

Put apples into greased, shallow baking dish. Blend remaining ingredients to a mealy consistency; sprinkle over apples. Bake at 375°F. 30 to 40 minutes. Cut into squares. Serve in small containers with snug fitting lids. Unused portions keep up to 5 days.

BAKED APPLES

3 baking apples
¼ cup boiling water
½ cup maple-blended syrup
¼ tsp. cinnamon

Core apples and place in baking dish and add water. Cover and bake in 375°F. oven for 35 minutes. Mix together syrup and cinnamon. Uncover apples and bake 20 minutes longer, basting several times with syrup-cinnamon mixture. Baste several more times while apples are cooling. Chill. To pack place an apple in paper bowl and wrap all in plastic wrap. Keeps 3 to 4 days.

Sweet Finales

CARAMEL JUNKET

2 cups milk
¹/₃ cup sugar
¹/₃ cup boiling water
1 junket tablet
Dash salt
1 tsp. vanilla

Heat milk until lukewarm. Carmelize sugar, add boiling water, and cook until syrup is reduced to ¹/₃ cup. Cool; slowly add milk to syrup. Crush junket tablet to fine powder and add to mixture along with salt and vanilla. Pour into serving-sized containers with tight fitting lids. Cool at room temperature until set, then chill.

COFFEE FLAVORED RICE PUDDING

1 cup packaged pre-cooked rice
1 cup coffee
1 cup raisins
¹/₂ cup chopped pecans
¹/₈ tsp. nutmeg
Dash of salt
¹/₂ cup packed brown sugar
1 cup heavy cream, whipped

Prepare rice according to package instructions, using coffee instead of water. Stir in remaining ingredients, except cream, and mix well. Chill.

Fold in whipped cream and carefully spoon into individual serving-sized containers with tight fitting lids. May be frozen.

CRANBERRY-PEAR TAPIOCA

¼ quick-cooking tapioca
3 Tbsp. sugar
Dash of ground cloves
2 cups cranberry juice cocktail
1 can (1 lb. 13-oz.) pears, drained and diced

Combine all ingredients, except pears, in saucepan. Mix well. Cook and stir over medium heat until mixture comes to a boil. Remove from heat. Cool, stirring occasionally. Fold in pears. Spoon into small containers with tight fitting covers and chill until used. Keeps up to 7 days.

FRUIT COMPOTE

1 pkg. (10-oz.) frozen raspberries, thawed
1 can (17-oz.) apricot halves
2 tsp. cornstarch
1 can (17-oz.) purple plums, drained

Drain raspberries and apricots, reserving syrups. Combine fruit syrups, adding enough water to make 1½ cups. Stir cornstarch into syrup mixture in saucepan and heat until mixture thickens. Add fruit; spoon into serving-sized containers with tight fitting lids. Chill. Keeps up to 6 days.

MOCHA DESSERT

1 pkg. (3½-oz.) vanilla pudding (not instant)
1 tsp. vanilla
2 tsp. instant coffee
1 cup semi-sweet chocolate chips

Prepare pudding according to label directions and add vanilla. Add coffee and chocolate chips; stir to dissolve. Spoon into serving-sized containers with tight fitting lids. Chill. Keeps up to 4 days.

Sweet Finales

PAPAYA FLUMMERY

3 medium-ripe papayas
¼ cup fresh lime juice
½ cup Orange juice
½ cup water
⅔ cup sugar
¼ cup tapioca

Peel papayas, halve remove seeds. Cut fruit into chunks, then puree in blender. Pour pureed fruit into saucepan and add remaining ingredients. Let stand 5 to 10 minutes. Place mixture over medium heat and bring to a full boil, stirring constantly. Cool slightly before spooning into individual serving containers with tight fitting lids. Make 4 servings. Keeps up to 6 days.

PINEAPPLE-BERRY BOWL

2½ cups pineapple chunks
1 pint fresh raspberries
1 pint fresh strawberries

Drain pineapple, reserving juice. In serving-sized containers arrange the strawberries, pineapple chunks, and raspberries. Pour chilled pineapple juice over fruit in each container, cover with lids, then chill. Keeps up to 5 days.

PUMPKIN CUSTARD

1 cup milk
1 cup canned pumpkin
½ cup sugar
1 tsp. cinnamon
½ tsp. nutmeg
½ tsp. vanilla
2 eggs, well beaten
Dash salt

Pour milk into eggs and beat together. Add rest of ingredients and beat slightly. Pour into custard pan and place in larger pan of water in oven. Bake 350ºF. 30 to 40 minutes. Spoon into individual serving containers. Cool, then chill. Keeps up to 5 days.

Sweet Finales

RHUBARB-STRAWBERRY TAPIOCA

¾ cup sugar
⅓ cup instant tapioca
¼ tsp. salt
2½ cups rhubarb, sliced
2 cups water
1½ cups strawberries, sliced

In saucepan stir together sugar, tapioca, and salt. Stir in rhubarb and water. Cook and stir over medium heat until rhubarb is tender and mixture is thickened. Remove from heat and stir in strawberries. Spoon into small containers with tight fitting lids. Chill. Unused servings will keep up to 5 days.

STRAWBERRIES IN WINE

1½ quarts strawberries
powdered sugar
Rose´ wine

Wash and hull berries and put into serving-sized containers with tight fitting lids. Sprinkle with sugar and add wine to almost cover berries. Refrigerate for several hours. Keeps up to 2 days.

Chapter 12

Menus in Minutes and More

MENUS IN MINUTES . . .

HOT LUNCHES

Bean Soup with Dumplings (page 135)
Sliced Avocado with Lemon Juice
Carrot Sticks
Mexican Chocolate (page 204)

Curried Eggs (page 148)
Applesauce
Dill Pickle
Rhubarb Crumb Cake (page 215) Hot Spiced Tea

Fish Chowder (page 138)
Oyster Crackers   Slices of Sharp Cheddar Cheese
Carrot Cole Slaw (page 247)
Baked Apple (page 227)
Hot Herb Tea

Menus in Minutes

Irish Stew (page 150)
Buttered Whole-Grain Bread
Raisin Tarts (page 216)
Hot Spiced Coffee (page 203)

Minestrone (page 141)
Bread Sticks
Antipasta (olives, cheese, Italian peppers,
hard-cooked eggs, etc.)
Fresh Pear or Apple   Chilled wine

Oriental Meat Balls (page 151)
Chow Mein Noodles
Green Pepper Slices
Applesauce   Fortune Cookies
Hot Green Tea

Southern B-B-Q Open Faces (page 145)
Potato Chips
Cherry Tomatoes   Carrot Sticks
Mayonnaise Cake (page 214)
Hot Spiced Tea

Taco Burgers (page 145)
Tortilla Chips
Black Olives   Avocado Slices
Caramel Junket (page 228)
Tea, Coffee or Milk

Tomato Rarebit (page 152)
Raw Carrot Sticks
Fruit Salad,
Packaged Cookies   Milk or Tea

Western Chili (page 153)
Corn Bread (page 248)
Orange and Apple Sections
Raisin-Oatmeal Cookies   Hot Spiced Cider (page 203)

COLD LUNCHES

Chicken Nuggets (page 124)
Three Bean Salad (page 250)
Soft Buttered Rolls
Rhubarb Crumb Cake (page 215)   Tea Sparkle (page 199)

Chilled Cream of Avocado Soup (page 111)
Egg and Watercress Sandwich (page 14)
Carrot and Cucumber Sticks
Apple Bread   Iced Tea or Milk

Chilled Cream of Tomato Soup (page 50)
He-Man Shrimp Salad (page 117)
Sour Dough Rolls
Fresh Orange Cake (page 212)   Beverage

Roast Beef Salad (page 76)
Corn Chips
Mayonnaise Cake (page 214)   Tea Lemonade (page 198)

Sardine Sandwiches (page 17)
Carrot Cole Slaw (page 247)
Potato Chips   Large Dill Pickle
Ruby Red Consomme or Tomato Juice Cocktail
(page 206 and 199)
Walnut Chews (page 225)

Pickled Salmon (page 128)
Buttered Pumpernickle Bread
Fresh Mushroom Caps   Green Pepper Strips
Fresh Apple Drink (page 193)

Potato-Bacon Custard (page 129)
Fresh Apple, Peach, etc.
Quick and Easy Loafer's Cake (page 214)
Tomato Juice Cocktail (page 199)

Shrimp-Tomato Aspic (page 121)
Wheat Crackers
Cold Sliced Melon
Lemon Squares (page 224)   Fresh Apple Drink (page 193)

Zucchini Quiche (page 132)
Small Tossed Salad
Fruit Compote (page 229)
Pink Wine Blossom (page 197)

LOW-CALORIE LUNCHES

Boston Clam Chowder 61 cal. (page 53)
2 Saltines 68 cal.
Apple Slaw 61 cal. (page 61)
Maple Custard 90 cal. (page 66)
Lemon-Mint Tea (page 51)

Total Calories: 280

Menus in Minutes   236

Chilled Pineapple Meat Loaf   184 cal. (page 55)
Marinated Mushrooms   30 cal. (page 62)
½ of 5" dia. chilled cantaloupe   38 cal.
Egg Custard   55 cal. (page 64)
Iced Tea

Total Calories: 307

Hamburger-Vegetable Soup   130 cal. (page 56)
Vegetable Slaw   80 cal. (page 62)
1 Cup Water Packed Pears   75 cal.
1 Cup Unsweetened Grapefruit Juice   90 cal.

Total Calories: 375

Jellied Veal Loaf   109 cal. (page 57)
Bean and Beet Salad   55 cal. (page 61)
Fresh Peach Paradise   90 cal. (page 64)
Iced Tea or Diet Beverage

Total Calories: 254

Shrimp Salad   200 cal. (page 58)
6 Canned Asparagus Spears   22 cal.
1 Cup Fresh Strawberries   55 cal.
Anise-Cinnamon Tea (page 49)

Total Calories: 277

Chilled Tomato Bouillon   72 cal. (page 137)
Teriyaki Chicken   160 cal. (page 59)
1 Cup Fresh Diced Pineapple   74 cal.
2 Vanilla Wafers   44 cal.
Diet Beverage, Coffee, or Tea

Total Calories: 350

Menus in Minutes

Tomato Stuffed with Crab   103 cal. (page 60)
4 Saltine Crackers   68 cal.
1 Large Dill Pickle   15 cal.
Carrot-Pineapple Cocktail   84 cal. (page 49)

Total Calories: 325

HEALTHFUL LUNCHES

Avocado-Swiss Sandwich (page 159)
Soybean Nuts (page 168)
Fresh Fruit
Prune Pudding (page 174)
Unsweetened Grapefruit Juice

Greek Stuffed Tomato (page 160)
Hominy Spoon Bread (page 166)
Fresh Pear or Apple
Banana Soy Milk (page 157)

Lentil Loaf (page 160)
Assorted Raw Vegetables
Chilled Melon
Indian Pudding (page 172)
Fresh Tomato Juice (page 157)

Navy Bean Soup (page 161)
Cheddar Whole-Wheat Bread (page 165)
Tart Apple
Molasses-Nut Custard (page 173)   Carrot Juice (page 157)

Nut-Cheese Patties (page 161)
Pear and Apple Wedges
Prune Brown Bread (page 167)
Orange Buttermilk Nog (page 158)

Raw Vegetables with Dip (page 168)
Sliced Caraway Cheese
Whole-Wheat Crackers
Chilled Seedless Grapes
Orange Buttermilk Nog (page 158)

Tabuli (page 162)
Carrot and Cucumber Sticks
Raw Cashews
Carob Caramels (page 171)
Green Drink (page 158)

Vitality Soup (page 163)
Steamed Corn Bread (page 169)
Square of Natural Cheddar Cheese
Fruit Filled Orange (page 172)   Herb Tea with Honey

QUICK LUNCHES

Banana-Nut Sandwich (page 11)
Potato Chips
Black Olives   Sweet Pickle
Cookies   Milk or Juice

Cheesy-Tuna Chowder (page 136)
Crackers
Fruit Cocktail   Packaged Peanut Butter Cookies
Milk

Chicken-Avocado Toss (page 114)
Assorted Crackers
Fresh Fruit   Packaged Pudding
Beverage

Sardine Sandwiches (page 17)
Three Bean Salad (page 250)
Hard-Cooked Egg
Fresh Fruit
Beverage

Savory Meat Loaf (page 31)
Lemon Broth (page 204)
Carrot and Celery Sticks
Beverage

Roquefort-Liverwurst Sandwiches (page 16)
Packaged Chips
Dill Pickle   Applesauce (page 33)
Packaged Cookies   Tea of Milk

Tuna-Sprout Salad (page 121)
Sesame or Corn Chips
Melon Cocktail (page 34)
Lemon Pound Cake (page 43)
Beverage

Turkey-Pocket Sandwiches (page 86)
Cranberry Sauce (page 34)
Fresh Orange
Maraschino Cake (page 43)   Beverage

Quick Corned Beef B-B-Q (page 144)
Carrot Sticks and Cherry Tomatoes
Peaches in Syrup (page 35)   Packaged Cookies
Beverages

KIDS' LUNCHES

Chili Spaghetti (page 179)
Carrot Sticks
Gingerbread Cupcake (page 188)   Milk or Juice

Corn-Crisped Drumsticks (page 179)
Cheesy Potato Salad (page 184)
Celery Sticks   Dill Pickle
Raspberry Flip

Creamed Chicken Over Rolls (page 180)
Carrot-Raisin Salad (page 183)
Fresh Fruit
Caramel Popcorn Ball (page 187)   Milk

Hot Dogs (page 180)
Mock Baked Beans (page 185)
Potato Chips
Peanut Butter Cookies (page 189)
Milk

Macaroni 'n Cheese Salad (page 180)
Buttered Bread
Vegetable Sticks
Cookies   Carrot Milk (page 177)

Peanut Butter Banana Sandwich (page 181)
Corn Chips
Cheese Stuffed Celery
Cream of Tomato Soup (page 55)
Cookies   Milk

Pronto Spaghetti (page 181)
Waldorf Salad (page 186)
Buttered French Bread
Pudding   Milk

Ravioli Soup (page 182)
Saltine Crackers
Pineapple Coleslaw (page 186)
Macaroons (page 189)   Milk

Tacos (page 182)
Fresh Fruit
Chocolate Chip Cookies (page 187)
Maple-Nut Milk (page 177)

ELEGANT LUNCHES

Antipasta Roll-ups (page 89)
Italian Peppers   Olives   Green Onions
Bread Sticks
Strawberries Sprinkled with Confectioner's Sugar   Chilled Rose'

Artichoke Fritatta (page 90)
Tossed Salad
Sour Dough Rolls
Lemon-Cheese Pudding   Red Wine

Beef Bourguignonne (page 90)
Hard Crusted Rolls
Tomato Stuffed with Artichoke (page 103)
Fresh Fruit Salad   Sparkling Wine

Bouillabaisse
Crusty French Bread
Monterey Jack Cheese
Fresh Fruit   White Wine

Cheese and Onion Pie (page 91)
Tossed Salad
Pickled Herring
Marmalade Fruit Combo (page 106)   Burgundy

Chilled Ham and Leek Quiche (page 92)
Chilled Lemon Carrots (page 247)
Pickled Zucchini (page 250)
Sherry Chiffon Pie   Rose' Frappe'

Curried Chicken Mousse (page 94)
Assorted Crackers
Thinly Sliced Swiss Cheese
Pecan Tarts (page 107)   White Wine

Moussaka (page 98)
Pickled Zucchini (page 250)   Pickled Green Beans (page 249)
Feta Cheese   Greek Olives
Dark Bread
Marmalade Fruit Combo (page 106)   White Wine

Shrimp Steamed in Beer (page 99)
Sharp Cheese   Hard Crusted Rolls
Carrot Coleslaw
Chocolate Cheesecake
Dark Beer

Stuffed Eggs Royal (page 102)
Caviar Stuffed Artichoke (page 103)
Pickled Green Beans (page 249)   Crab Stuffed Celery (page 117)
Fresh Fruit   White Wine

Menus in Minutes

MAKE AHEAD LUNCHES

Cheesy Hash Turnovers (page 24)
Mustard Mixed with Sesame Seeds
(for dipping turnovers)
Carrot and Celery Sticks
Fresh Fruit
Maraschino Cake (page 43)   Tea Sparkle (page 199)

Cold Curried Chicken Loaf (page 25)
Dinner Roll
Bonanza Salad (page 33)
Applesauce (page 33)   Chocolate Cookies (page 40)
Beverage

Cold Poached Fish Fillets with
Cocktail Sauce (page 26)
Whole-Wheat Crackers
Chunk of Swiss Cheese
Bran and Date Muffin (page 39)
Spiced Iced Coffee (page 198)

Crab or Shrimp Salad (page 94)
Pickled Beets (page 35)   Applesauce (page 33)
Lemon Pound Cake (page 43)
Milk or Tea

Fracadeller (page 28)
Corn Chips
Rhubarb Sauce (page 36)   Nutmeg Cake (page 44)
Beverage

Iced Cream of Vegetable Soup (page 28)
Corned Beef Sandwich (page 26)
Golden Fruit Compote (page 34)
Honey-Raisin Quick Bread (page 42)
Beverage

Lemon Salmon Steaks (page 29)
Relish Salad (page 35)   Melon Cocktail (page 34)
Apricot-Cream Cheese Bread   Milk or Tea

Roast Beef Sandwiches (page 30)
Relish Salad (page 35)
Packaged Chips
Peaches in Syrup (page 35)   Apple Rolls (page 37)
Beverage

Super Dagwood (page 32)
Potato Chips
Cranberry Sauce (page 34)
Maraschino Cake (page 43)   Beverage

Sweet and Sour Chicken Wings (page 32)
Dinner Roll
Bonanza Salad (page 33)
Cheesecake (page 39)   Beverage

AND MORE . . .

CARROT COLESLAW

1 cup cabbage, shredded
½ cup carrots, shredded
1 Tbsp. parsley, minced
¼ cup mayonnaise
½ Tbsp. lemon juice
½ tsp. salt
¼ tsp. sugar

Combine all ingredients. Cover and chill. Will keep up to 4 days. (serves 4)

CHILLED LEMON CARROTS

1 lb. carrots, pared and sliced
½ tsp. salt
1 cup water
2 Tbsp. margarine
1 lemon, thinly sliced
¾ cup maple-blended syrup

Combine carrots with salt and water in frying pan. Heat to boiling. Cook 10 minutes; uncover and cook 3 minutes longer. Add margarine, lemon slices, and syrup. Cook slowly, turning carrots several times, 20 minutes until richly glazed. Drain excess liquid and discard lemons. Chill.

Menus in Minutes

COCONUT-CARROT SALAD

1 cup flaked coconut
1½ cups shredded carrots
¼ cup raisins
2 Tbsp. lemon juice
½ tsp. ground ginger
¼ cup mayonnaise
1 can mandarin orange sections, drained

Combine all ingredients in bowl and mix well. Chill. Spoon serving portion into plastic container with tight fitting lid. Remainder will keep up to 3 days. (serves 4)

CORN BREAD

5 Tbsp. melted margarine
1 cup sifted flour
¼ cup sugar
1 Tbsp. baking powder
½ tsp. salt
1 cup yellow corn meal
1 egg, well beaten
1 cup milk

Sift together flour, sugar, baking powder, and salt. Mix in corn meal. Make a well in center of dry ingredients; pour in shortening, milk, and egg. Beat until just smooth, being careful not to over-mix. Spoon into greased 8 x 8 x 2" pan. Bake at 425°F. for 15 to 20 minutes.

CRAB STUFFED CELERY

1 can crab meat
1 pkg. (3-oz.) cream cheese
1 tsp. onion juice
Deep-grooved celery sticks

Mix all ingredients together; stuff celery and store in refrigerator (up to 3 days) until ready to use.

KIDNEY-BEAN SALAD

1 can (16-oz.) kidney beans, drained
2 Tbsp. tarragon vinegar
1 Tbsp. lemon juice
¼ cup parsley, finely chopped
½ tsp. salt
½ cup celery, diced
1 large onion, thinly sliced
2 hard-cooked eggs, chopped
2 Tbsp. mayonnaise

Combine first 6 ingredients and chill 1 hour. Add remaining ingredients and pack into plastic containers with tight fitting lids. Keeps up to 3 days. (serves 4)

PICKLED GREEN BEANS

2 lbs. green beans
1¾ cup white vinegar
1½ cup water
¾ cup sugar
4 tsp. salt
1 Tbsp. mustard seed
1 Tbsp. whole black pepper
1 cinnamon stick
2 cloves garlic, minced
3 small onions, peeled and sliced

Cook beans in boiling water until tender crisp. Drain. Add vinegar, water, sugar, and salt. Tie mustard seed, pepper and cinnamon in bag. Bring vinegar mixture to boil. Add onions. Simmer 15 minutes. Continue simmering while packing sterilized jars one at a time. Vinegar mixture should cover beans. Seal. (makes 3 pints)

Menus in Minutes

PICKLED ZUCCHINI

Pint screw top jars
3 to 4 small zucchini
3 Tbsp. olive oil
2 Tbsp. olive oil
2 cloves garlic, quartered
½ tsp. Oregano
¼ tsp. salt
1 bay leaf
Wine vinegar

Wash and trim ends from squash. Cut crosswise into ¼" slices.
Heat 3 Tbsp. oil in skillet. Add zucchini and cook slowly until browned. Drain on paper towels. Cool and place in jars. Combine 2 Tbsp. oil, garlic, oregano, salt, and bay. Pour over zucchini and fill jar to ¼" from top with vinegar. Screw cap onto jar and store in refrigerator at least 24 hours. Serve cold.

THREE BEAN SALAD

1 can yellow wax beans
1 can kidney beans
1 can green beans
½ cup salad oil
½ tsp. salt
¾ cup sugar
1 green pepper, thinly sliced
1 red onion, thinly sliced
¼ tsp. pepper
½ cup vinegar

Drain beans. Mix all ingredients together. Refrigerate 3 to 4 hours or overnight. Keeps up to 10 days.

1. When making layer cakes for the lunch sack, sandwich frosting between layers.
2. A damp paper towel wrapped in plastic wrap or foil is excellent for aftermeal clean-ups.
3. Don't forget to pack heavier items on bottom of lunch sack or box.
4. Two paper napkins are better than one.
5. Lunch supplies and equipment are best kept in one place, preferably near working surface.
6. Prepare sandwich fillings, cold entree, cookies, or desserts in advance.
7. Vary shapes of crisp raw vegetables for added interest and attractiveness (i.e., radish roses, celery or carrot curls).
8. Send along a small shaker of salt and pepper.
9. Children love surprise apples — remove core and stuff with dates, paper wrapped candy, nuts, raisins, etc.
10. A small box of raisins makes a welcome treat.
11. Greeting cards for special occasions make a nice addition to the lunch box.
12. Vary the butter or margarine used in sandwich making by adding parsley, onion, dried herbs, garlic, honey, etc.
13. Vary the form of sandwich by constructing doubledeckers, cutting out various shapes, rolling them up, or forming contrasts with light and dark bread.
14. Accompany a thermos of hot water with different flavored bags of herb tea and small packets of honey.
15. Frozen seafood cocktails make great lunch bag tuck-ins (they'll thaw by lunchtime).
16. Shelled nuts, cheese stuffed celery, dried fruits, popcorn, or corn chips make welcome lunch time treats.
17. Choose foods which can be handled easily and eaten quickly.
18. Wash out lunch boxes and thermos bottles thoroughly every night.
19. Keep on hand waxed paper, paper napkins, paper or plastic containers with lids, paper hot drink cups, plastic spoons and forks, and lunch-sized bags.
20. Clean raw vegetables, wash fruit, and prepare the makings of a salad the night before.

Menus in Minutes

21. Try to include two different kinds of sandwiches with each lunch.
22. Be generous with sandwich fillings, but don't allow filling to ooze out over the edges of sandwiches.
23. Keep a supply of canned meats on hand for lunch bag use.
24. Tie a cooked frankfurter on a string and float in thermos of hot soup.

INDEX

Beef

Index

Beverages

Index

Breads

Cakes

Candy

Cheese

Index

Chicken

Cookies and Bars

Index

Eggs

Fish

Shell Fish

Fruit

Index

Game Hens

Lamb

Muffins

Index

Pies

Pork

Index

Puddings

Salads

Sandwiches

Index   264

Snacks

Index   266

Soups

Index

Turkey

Vegetables

Quiche

Index